Through a Daddy's Eyes

Journal of a Stay At Home Dad

By

Mark S. Major

AmErica House
Baltimore

ISBN: 1-58851-920-1
PUBLISHED BY AMERICA HOUSE BOOK PUBLISHERS
www.publishamerica.com
Baltimore

Printed in the United States of America

To: Lisa

" I Am Glad We
Have Become Friends
And I Hope You Enjoy
My Book "

Mark

3-22-02

Introduction

Me

I am a 31-year-old male, with a good job with the third largest food service company in the US, and I just quit. What? I just quit my job. I do not have another job, a better job with more money and I am not going back to school to earn my masters. What am I thinking? Oh yeh, I quit to stay at home and raise my 2 daughters. Am I crazy or was this just destiny?

I grew up for 21 years in a typical southern suburb of Chicago. I have an older sister and an older brother. We are all 4 years apart. To be honest we are not very close with each other or have anything in common. I love them, we can rely each other in the event one of us needs another, but besides holidays or special events, I rarely see them. It was no accident we had our children 23 months apart, I grew up not knowing my brother and sister, so I want my children to be close. I am envious of friends of mine who have brothers and sisters close in age, who are very goods friends with each other. I pray my 2 daughters become the best of friends, rather than just sisters.

My mom stayed home with us, while my father worked downtown. He took the train everyday back and forth from work. I loved it. Why. Most fathers you don't know when they will be home. Not my dad. Everyday at 6:15 p.m. he would walk through that door. It is a great feeling not having to ask my mom everyday "when's dad coming home", because I knew at 6:15 pm he would be home. I am very much like my dad but would never admit it to anyone. We both do a lot around the house, love going to the hardware store, just to go, and what should be a 5 minute job, takes and hour. As I grow up and raise my family, I see so much of my dad in me I think to myself, "hey, that's not a bad thing at all".

My mom, well, was exactly that, a mom. She took good care of us as best as she could. It must have been hard with 3 kids 4 years apart in different stages of life. While I was in diapers, my sister who would have been 8 was probably just starting to notice boys. My brother who would have been 4 was probably just starting to learn to burn things. My mom tried very hard; did laundry on Mondays, cleaned the house on Fridays, and cooked everyday. That was the bad part. As hard as she tried, my mom wasn't a very good cook. It wasn't like prison food or anything, she was just one of those moms

5

who didn't use a lot of spices, or cook anything unusual. It got pretty bad when we got older because we were old enough now to realize that the food my mom prepared wasn't very good and we often got vocal about it. My mother often cried because of us kids. We let her have it many times about her cooking or the cloths she might have bought for us, but as I said before, she tried. Maybe that is why to this day, I do all the cooking and buy my own clothes.

Growing up was very typical. I had a lot of friends. I was in Boy Scouts and even made it all the way to be an eagle scout. In high school I was on the swim team and the tennis team. I was just average in swimming but very good in tennis. I won several tournaments playing singles, and in my senior year I went to the state championship tournament as a doubles team. During high school I also worked full time. At age 15, I got my first job at Kentucky Fried Chicken. It was a great learning experience and the money at the time seemed like a million dollars. I believe I made $3.20 an hour. I used to bring home all the left over chicken and potatoes to my friends' houses and their mothers would love me. I fed a lot of families the short time I worked there. I then worked for a Mexican restaurant called Chi Chi's. I worked 40 hours a week, went to school, and played in sports. I had to. I loved sports, but I also needed the money to put away for college. I would work there all the way through high school until I went away to college.

College. "The fountain of knowledge, everyone learns how to drink." Probably the best four years of my entire life, and probably will be. Four years of being strictly on your own, no work, 3 hours of class a day, and you don't even have to go if you don't want. Whoever thought of this college thing knew what he or she was talking about. I majored in communications with a minor in business. I was an average student as you can imagine but did graduate on time in 4 years. College probably can be summed in 3 words beginning all with the letter b: Beers, babes, and barf.

After college, reality of life hit hard. I was back at home with my parents, unemployed, flat broke and my girlfriend was still in college for another year. After awhile I got a job selling radio ads over the phone. That lasted about 4 months. Then I decided to become a stockbroker. Took my series 7 exam, passed it, and went to work for a brokerage firm. After about 3 months, our firm lost a lawsuit of 13 million and was forced to close. Unemployed again. Other firms called me regarding my services but I didn't want to see that happen to me all over again.

So I did what most guys would do. I visited my girlfriend a lot at college. She was only 2 hours away by car, so at least I was still able to drink and have a good time without the hassles of my parents. That Christmas I asked her to marry me. She of course said yes and we planned to marry in 18 months. She graduated in May and received a job with Motorola one week after graduation. Here I am one year out of college and still unemployed and she gets a job in a week. Destiny. So we packed and moved north about an hour away to start our life together. Of course I went with her. What was I supposed to do. Sit at home unemployed and plan our wedding alone. So while she worked I looked for a job, but for some reason all the good jobs were already taken by the time I got up at noon. Four months went by as I stayed home cooking and cleaning. Destiny. Finally I found a job with a collections agency. It was fun for awhile. At least I was able to kick butt instead of kiss butt to earn my commission. I quit the day before we got married. After our honeymoon I found a job right away. It was with a leasing company doing collections for them. This was a lot different type of collections than from the agency. I had to be polite and work with the deadbeats because they were our customers and potential future customers. I worked there for 3 and a half years. I then joined the finance department for the food service company I recently retired from. That could be the last job I ever have. Destiny. I believe that things in life happen for a reason. For the turn of events to happen the way they did in my life so far, it was destiny for me to stay home and raise my family.

Lisa

My true love in life. If there is such a thing as a soul mate, Lisa is that. We just celebrated our 7th wedding anniversary, but I have known and dated Lisa for over 19 years.

We met when I was in the 8th grade, she was in 7th. It was in the hall of our middle school when I introduced myself in front of her history class. I remember this like it was yesterday because the bell rang for class to begin, and of course I was not in my class, but trying to score on a babe. Her teacher came out of the classroom and grabbed my hair and pulled me away from Lisa. What a minute. Why didn't he pull her hair for her to get into class, I wasn't even in his classroom? Oh well, she felt sorry for me and from that day forward, began the rest of lives together.

We began to date off and on through junior high, high school and college. We lost our virginity to each other. We are very different people, opposites do attract. She was a straight A student, I was a B-minus or C-plus at best.

She studied; I went to rock concerts. I was fun, she was boring. I taught her how to have fun, she taught me how to love.

I honestly say we rarely fight. When we do, it lasts about 10 minutes, and I am the one usually apologizing. The fights are about nothing, sometimes not even worth the fight. Fighting is good in a relationship. It shows emotions and shows you care.

Lisa has a great career ahead of her. She graduated from college with honors in finance and wasted no time getting her MBA. She has been with Motorola since graduation, and probably will be for life. It just made sense for me to quit and raise our daughters with so much going for her. She thanks me everyday for what I have done because it makes her day so much more pleasant knowing the girls are left at home with their Daddy. That makes me happy knowing the trust she has in me raising her two daughters. They are her colors in the rainbow.

As a mother, she is the best. She puts them in front of everything, even me. I get frustrated and moan a lot when I need attention too. She gives it to me when she is able, and it is worth the wait. Her girls adore her as I do, and as people go, she is as perfect as they come. She is my life, she is my world, I would be nothing without her.

McKenzie

Our first born. I will never forget her birthday or time of birth. She was born at 5:30am on May 30th, 1996, or five-thirty at five-thirty. She was actually due on May 29th, but there was an incident.

Lisa began her contractions on May 28th. We went into the hospital and spent the day. With no movement we were sent home. The next day we went to the doctors office because she was still contracting. The doctor couldn't feel the head, only the butt. The baby was breach. We went to the hospital for an ultrasound and an x-ray to confirm his prognosis and sure enough, butt first. We had the option to try to deliver naturally or have a caesarean birth. We agreed to give it a try naturally. Eighteen hours later, by caesarean birth, Lisa gave birth to the most beautiful baby girl ever born, McKenzie Renee Major. With her feet above her head, poop coming out of her butt, covered in blood, she looked like a girl only a mother and father could love. And we do very much.

She is currently 2 years and 4 months old and I would take 500 just like her, well maybe 2 or 3.

Josie

Our 2nd daughter. Born almost 23 months after McKenzie. She was born on April 24th, 1998. I will remember her birthday by "we had one more on four-twenty four."

Unlike McKenzie, Josie was no surprise. We found out the sex at 28 weeks. We loved her at that moment. We decided to find out for many reasons. One we couldn't wait, and we wanted to get the bedroom ready before-hand. It was fun to tell people we knew, but wouldn't tell them. It really made people mad. It was great. Even though she wasn't a surprise, she was difficult.

We had an ultrasound done at 36 weeks to make sure she wasn't breech like her sister. She was already to go naturally and Lisa was nervous. After her caesarean, she didn't mind it. But we decided if possible, we were going to try a natural birth. We were admitted into the hospital at 7 am. Lisa was dilated 2 centimeters. Things looked good. At noon she was 4 centimeters and Lisa got her epidural. I don't blame her. If you can do anything without pain, I see no reason why you shouldn't. Some people would argue that with drugs it is not a true natural delivery, but I am sure these are the same people who go to the dentist and get novocaine for a filling.

At 2 pm she was still only about 5 centimeters dilated so they gave her Pitocin. At 6 pm she was still at 5 centimeters and the doctors were concerned because Lisa was running a fever and didn't want to risk a virus in the placenta. Lisa felt a lot of pressure as the baby wanted to come out but she was still far away from being able to push. At 8:00 pm, Josie Samantha was born, caesarean birth. She looked a little blue and Lisa was in a lot of pain. On one hand I have a wife who has just been through hell and back, lying on a table crying in pain, and on the other hand I have a brand new baby daughter, who isn't breathing right and tubes are being stuck down he throat. I felt completely helpless and lost. I was torn between my wife and my baby. I decided to stay by my wife's side until she was at least comfortable. I knew that Josie was in very good hands and there was nothing I could do for her at this time. Once Lisa was out of the operating room, I went to Josie's side. She was breathing only 75 percent oxygen and was under a breathing tent. They said because she was in the birth channel so long, she swallowed too much fluid and is having difficulty breathing. I kept going back and forth from my wife to my daughter, checking on them both. I never told Lisa what was going on, I didn't want to upset her in her condition. It was the single worst day of my life as Lisa and I swore to each other that we would have no more children after this ordeal. Lisa did catch a virus in labor, and tests were being done on Josie to see if she also had the virus. After 2 days of the breathing

9

tent, Josie was breathing all on her own. She never caught the virus and was able to go home on time with us after 4 long days in the hospital. That day made me very humble and made me realize there is nothing in this world that is worth more to me than the love I have for my wife, Lisa.

Brodie

Our family dog. We have had her now 6 years. She is a mutt, part keeshond, and part terrier. Lisa just insisted from the day we bought our house that she wanted a dog. Didn't care what it was. Whenever we went into a pet store she wanted whatever was the cutest. So one day I bought her Brodie. She was only 6 weeks old and I have to admit, pretty damn cute. We treated Brodie like the first born she was. She had it better than most humans have. Brodie was in heaven until McKenzie came. Four years living like a queen, now she is in the doghouse. Lisa hates her and wants to get rid of her. I have to keep reminding her she was the one that wanted her, so if she wants her gone, she will have to do it. Well, Lisa is a wimp and will not get rid of her. So I feed her well and we can only hope for the best.

Monday

My first day of being a full-time dad. Am I excited or too nervous to tell? My first mission is the grocery store. Scenario: a 2 year old, a 5 month old and what do you know, it's is pouring out. I guess God is going to test my patience very early. I pull in and park in the first spot. Yes! I carry both children under my arms while holding an umbrella. Everything was going well until I stepped in a puddle and now I have one wet foot and a long day ahead of me. We make it in the store, shake off like a dog and grab a cart. I put my little one in the front, while my 2 year old begs for a cookie from a demonstrator. As I begin to shop, I begin to get looks from others. "What is he doing with two children in a grocery store," people must be thinking. Or, "he must be getting punished by his wife having to do the shopping," I have been telling myself that whatever people will say or think about me staying at home while my wife works will not bother me, but now that I am in the situation, I do begin to feel out of place. I will have to learn to overcome this and I am sure in time, I will.

As we check out, an employee, an older man, comes up to me and asks me if I need help. I usually will say no, but "yes" came out of my mouth before he even finished his sentence. I pushed the cart with the groceries and the employee buttoned up McKenzie's rain coat and held her hand to the van. While I strapped my kids in, he unloaded the groceries in the pouring rain into the back. I have learned a valuable lesson on my first day. When you have children, you can get people to do things for you and take advantage of it, I know I will every time.

Tuesday

On Tuesdays and Thursdays I get a break in the morning. McKenzie goes to the Montessori School in the morning from 8:45 am to 11:00 am. Well it happened. As we were waiting for class to open, I was sitting there with my baby and another mother comes up to me and says "Oh we have the baby today," and my reply was "everyday," she then states "oh, a stay at home dad." No just a dad. I never heard my mother described as a "stay at home mom." I thought it wouldn't bother me, but it does. I must get over it. Then she tells me I must join her women's group...Women's group. Duh, I'm a man. Since this is the decade of political correctness, if I join the name must be changed to "parental group." Plus I would like to find out what happens when the husbands find out there wives will be hanging out with a man during the day, a good- looking one too.

Wednesday

A fight. Can you believe it? After only 3 days at being at home my wife picks a fight with me. I couldn't believe it. She picks fights with me only after 3 days. Why, because the night before I went to bed at 9:30 pm and she still had laundry to fold and she gets no breaks. Hello. This is a woman who left the house at 7:30 am and returned at 6:00 pm. Since she was gone I had taken care of the children all day, did the ironing, drove back and forth twice to school, made dinner, did the dishes and cleaned the house. I was tired, give me a break. My wife has only 2 responsibilities outside of her work. That is the laundry on Sundays and writes out bills. I tell her what the bills are and when to pay them and she writes them out. It has always been this way. My duties include, even when I was working full time I add, was to cook, do the dishes, cut the lawn, shovel snow, gas up the cars, all other outside work, make the bed, etc. etc. I try to do as much because I know she works hard at work. But the nerve of her getting on my case about going to bed early. I couldn't believe it. She was acting, should I say it, like a "man." Just because she works all day at the office doesn't mean she is not going to pull her weight at home. After a lengthy discussion, in which a lot of four-letter words flew around, we kissed, made up and even had sex. It is true what the say; make up sex is some of the best sex there is.

Friday

The next 2 days went on as scheduled. Friday, McKenzie and I cut the lawn while Josie took her morning nap. It is nice to have some time alone with my oldest to bond with her. She loves to help Daddy, even though she is making it harder on me whatever she may be doing, but I tell her what a big helper she is and she is so proud.

There are many sacrifices we are going to have to take now that we are down to one income. We have to budget everything and plan well ahead. We went to the mall later that night as a family, and there were plenty of things we wanted to buy, but couldn't. My wife was a little depressed but she told me by the look in my eyes everyday she comes home and sees how happy I am, and how happy the children are having Daddy home is worth more than the weight of gold. After my first week of being at home with my children, the laughs and cries we shared, the next 51 weeks couldn't come fast enough.

Week 2
Oct 12th-16th

Monday

Only after a week with the kids full-time, and I am now missing the things in life I took for granted. Things I did with ease and to my enjoyment. Now, things in life are much more difficult for people with children, then for people without. For example, talking on the phone. As soon as I get on the phone, McKenzie automatically asks, "who is it," then she says, "let me say hi," then while I am trying to have a conversation, she is pulling my leg and saying "say goodbye Daddy," after years of being able to hold a conversation on the phone, I am now limited to about a whole 2 minutes before I have to hang up, and I am sure the person on the other line is grateful for that. It would be easier for people to write me than to call. Televison. Nothing better than sitting on the couch with the remote and switching channels. Now. I went from watching ESPN Sportscenter, or any other sporting event ever created, an occasional situation comedy and of course, the Playboy Channel to watching Barney! My daughter is hooked on Barney. Not only do I get to watch Barney twice a day, but the four little fat, ugly, colored animals called Teletubbies. I basically have lost all existence to the outside world. I make sure the first thing I do in the morning is grab my paper, find out what date it is and make sure the still live in a free world. Another is eating. I cannot sit down and eat with McKenzie asking "what you eating" and eventually eat all that I was going to eat. I will definitely lose weight while at home. I have to sneak food upstairs or eat it out of her sight for me to get anything down my throat. I swear she is part panther and should hunt for her food because no matter where I may be hiding, she finds me and devours my food. The last is what I miss the most. It is, and was, the only true peace a man encounters during the day. The shrine, or the library, or the office, or whatever people may call it, but my days of going to the bathroom and enjoying a peaceful bowel movement are completely over. I used to go to work and take my paper in there and be able to read the entire sports section before having to return to my desk. Now, I am able to just about get it all out before I have to pull up my pants and run to find out what the screaming and crying is all about. I try to hold it in for when they might be sleeping, but no way. I am a morning depositor and I have to go when the coffee meets my bladder. I am not asking for much. An occasional conversation without being interrupted 300 times trying to find out "who it is", or eating my lunch, by myself, or watching a ball game beside a purple dinosaur. But the one thing that hurts the most that I had to give up, my time alone between me and the bowl.

Wednesday

I was on a mission today to find a Halloween costume and a red wagon. First of all, I thought a red wagon was about as easy to find as say a gallon of milk. I went to store after store after store and no red wagon. I need this wagon because I am taking Josie's six month picture in it with all her bears but I could not find a wagon. I called all my friends who have children and none of them had one. I even went to some antique stores but no luck. Also, last night in the mail we received a refund check from the catalog we ordered McKenzie's Halloween costume from stating they are out of stock. Out of stock! How can you advertise something when you don't have any. Not very pleased. She was going to be a ladybug. By mistake we have told her and she has been telling everyone that she is going to be a ladybug for Halloween. It is now 2 weeks before Halloween and no ladybug costume and you guessed it, my wife is in a panic. So I take it upon myself and first thing in the morning I grabbed both kids and headed up to super K-mart. Store is empty on I'm on a mission for a ladybug costume. I am up for the challenge. I get to the aisle of Halloween costumes, I search and search and I find a ladybug headset and wings, but no body suit. Just my luck, I found half a costume. But before I have an anxiety attack, I search again. Nothing. Sweat begins to pour out of my head as I begin to imagine staying up all night sewing together a ladybug costume for my daughter. When all was about lost I noticed a Mini Mouse costume that had a ladybug body-suit in it instead of Mini Mouse. So like any good father would do I tore apart the mini mouse costume, pulled out the ladybug body suit, reassembled the package with the wings and headpiece and my mission is complete. My wife will be very pleased with me. I can sense we will be having sex tonight. One down, one to go. The red wagon. I am hot now, so I am feeling good. We head over to the toys and there it is. One lonely red rider wagon. I was jumping up and down like I won the lottery. Well I did. Because not only did I find a ladybug costume but also the red wagon for Josie's six month picture. I am a good dad and I have proven I will do anything for my children , plus I am definitely getting sex tonight.

Friday

The end of my second week. It's a beautiful day, mid 70's for an October day is heaven. My daughters and I were outside the majority of the day. Being outside I have found is the key to staying sane. They can yell, run and not be in danger of breaking anything all of the time. Fresh air also tires them out, as nap time is very important, not only to them but to me. A neighbor of ours came over with her two daughters. They are just about the same age but a little older. We tried to go to the park. We made it ok, it's right across the street from my house. But as we were there enjoying ourselves for about a whole ten minutes, the school bell rang for lunch and about ten thousand (it seemed that many) screaming, yelling kids came out of the school and practically trampled all of us. I now know how it would be to run with the bulls in Spain and I have to say , I am going to take a pass. We grabbed all the kids and got out of there before any of us turned into pancakes.

As I am walking home, I am thinking how hard the winter months are going to be. I am desperately trying not to stick my kids in front of the TV. Yes, they do watch some TV. Mostly Barney, Arthur and Teletubbies. It comes out to be about two hours a day. I think that is not bad for an twelve hour day. If there is a mother or father who stays home all day and tells me that their children watches no TV during the day, I have to laugh and just not believe them. There is not enough to do during the day to occupy them all day without TV. If there is, I would love to know. I believe TV is good in moderation. Not only does it entertain the kids for awhile; it gives you a break to do something else. That is why I am dreading the winter months ahead. We won't be able to go out as much as we do now, and I am truly going to try to moderate the televison in-take. I must come up with activities for us to do, and hope I do not to turn out like Jack Nicholson did in *The Shining*.

With every passing week, my love grows stronger as I watch them grow, not alone, but with me, their Daddy.

Week 3
Oct 19th-23rd

Tuesday

Walking out the door isn't easy. It takes planning and strategy. I pretend I am a general in the army, and I am at war, I have a plan and strategy to win the battle. First, I have to coordinate our movements within the time frame of feedings and naps. I also must bring plenty of supplies: diapers, wipes, bibs, snacks, juice, milk and others to make it through the trenches. Then I must dress the troops for the weather at hand. Coats, shoes and hats are now in place, and even though I am now too tired from getting us ready, my plan of attack is mentally in hand. Loading and unloading the troops in and out of the vehicle takes muscle and patience. There is no time to waste, every second counts towards a potential defeat. The sweat and desire get me through in the nick of time. Just before the baby screams for milk, and the toddler is too tired to walk and wants to be carried, the conquest is over and we are safely at home. The battle has been won. As I look back, I may think to myself of ways of improving my movements, or decide if it was even worth going in the first place. But all in all, I survived. Until the next battle, which comes all too quick.

Thursday

Raising a 6-month-old and a 2-year-old is sometimes a crappy job, literally. As I was changing Josie's diaper, which had her digested carrots in it, she decides she is not done and shoots out a mud ball on Daddy's shirt. Isn't that special. All within minutes, McKenzie is on the potty doing her business and decides she doesn't need Daddy's help, so she wipes and gets dressed all by herself. After I clean myself off, I begin to smell a smell that smells very similar to crap, and yes, it's crap all over the toilet and on the floor and all over McKenzie's legs and butt. Today, was a crappy day, literally.

Friday

Some of my new vocabulary after 3 weeks:
"Whaty," my response to "Daddy" 400 times a day
"Night night," bedtime or nap time
"Pee pee," need to go to the bathroom
"Boo box," has snot in her nose and needs to get it out
"Blankey," blanket

I hope I never use these during any adult conversations.

It is nice being home and being able to do chores and projects during the week, that would usually need to be done on the weekends. My wife and I are noticing how much free time we have now on the weekends which allows us to do other things than run around doing chores. Our weekends used to be two days of catching up on things we couldn't do during the week. Now we are able to spend a lot more quality time with our daughters. During this past week alone, I was able to make wood gravestones for Halloween and place them in our front lawn. Last year, I never would have had the time to do it. Deciding to put my career on hold and stay home full time has paid dividends in my marriage, the welfare of my children, and me personally, which would surpass any stock on the stock market. No one can put a price on time, once it is gone, you can never get it back.

Week 4
Oct 26th-30th

Monday

A day off. Grandma came for the day to spend time with the girls. Thank god for grandmas. So I did what any other red blooded American should do on a picture perfect day, with temperatures in the mid 70's, I went out and played golf.

Tuesday

When I was getting mentally prepared for the challenge of staying home with a 2-year-old and a 4-month-old, I thought to myself the baby will be difficult at times, and the 2-year-old will be a piece of cake. I was wrong in my assumption. It is just the opposite. McKenzie is so much more high maintenance and demanding of my time than Josie. The crying, the changing of diapers and the never ending feedings has not taken a toll on me. She is a very good baby. Not that my older daughter isn't good, she is also very good. But from the time she wakes up, to the time she goes to bed, I am her personal servant. I really feel that way. Daddy is just a name. She is non-stop with the "Daddy." I don't know how many times a day I put her shoes and coat on and off. I wished we lived on a planet where we were all naked and didn't have to deal in clothing. She eats like a pregnant elephant. "I need a snack, I need a drink, I want this, I want that," all day long. I have to give in to her so she will be quiet and out of my hair so I can take care of Josie. You would figure you would need to attend to the baby first, than the toddler, but I have to get the bull tamed first, so I can care for the calf. Maybe that is why the second child is either more aggressive or more tame than the first. Josie has to always wait so patiently for Daddy to care for her. At times I feel so sorry for her but there is nothing I can do. In the long run, it is always better off waiting to care for Josie so I can do it right, and without interruption. By the third child, I am sure the parents just give up and the home becomes a free for all. Josie does have to fight harder for attention because I am so busy with McKenzie. It isn't fair, I know that, but there is nothing I can do. When McKenzie loses it, it is all over, then no one will get anything because Daddy will be taken away in an ambulance with men in white coats, and I will be resting peacefully in a rubber room with my bowl of jell-O.

Friday

It has now been one month since I quit my job to stay home full time with my children. What I have noticed in the past couple of weeks is that there is a "changing of the guard". What I mean by that is my role has changed from being just a "Dad", to more of a "Mom." Now that I am home, the tide has turned. I see myself doing more with them at night and on the weekends, that I have in the past when my wife and I worked. I have become accustomed to being their provider all day, and so have the children. In the past, no matter what, at night or on the weekends, even though we are both at home, McKenzie automatically go to "Mom" for this or "Mom" for that. Now, she seems to be going more to "Dad", rather than "Mom". It is not from a lack of love, or preference, I believe it is from routine. I am the one home all day doing everything for them. McKenzie more than likely will ask Daddy first before Mommy. When Josie is crying, I am able to hold her and comfort her to calm her down, I could never do that with McKenzie when she was a baby, only Mommy.

Even though I may have replaced "Mommy" on some of the routine tasks of childcare, I know, or never will, and never want to replace "Mommy." I have gotten closer to them than I ever had before, but there is no love or bond like mother-child. I can see the joy and love in their eyes and face when Mommy comes home. When they are sick, or sad, they always seem to want their Mommy, even though I am there. I am glad for that. I do not want to come first. As much as I love them, I always want them to want their Mommy more than me. I believe that is the way it should be. I might be the one home with them, but their Mommy is the one raising them. Nobody can replace "Mommy", no matter what the circumstances may be. You can put that in the bank.

Monday

Today I got a little taste of what it is going to be like with sick children. Not very delightful to say the least. On Friday of last week, Lisa brought Josie to see the doctor because she was very congested and had a cough. The doctor stated it is just a cold, not an ear infection, thank God, and just give her some over the counter medicine. On Monday she didn't seem any better. My day consisted of holding Josie all day as my back began to break little by little. By 5:30 pm I couldn't take it anymore and I had to page my wife to come home from work. I called the doctor's office and demanded a prescription. I didn't care what it was, I just wanted something. I went and got the prescription filled at 7 pm. Tomorrow better be a better day. I pray I never get sick. If McKenzie, Josie and myself get sick at the same time, Lisa better be afraid, very afraid.

Tuesday

Josie is feeling much better today. She is back to her own self and my back has been reprieved of duty. McKenzie, on the other hand was very sad today for some reason. As I was getting her ready for school, which she loves going to, she had tears in her eyes. She didn't want to go. McKenzie is a child in which when something gets in her head, it is very hard to get it out. She must have been thinking of something sad because nothing I said could change her mood. Since I was trying so hard to convince her that school is fun, just as I am about to pull out of the driveway I notice I still have by house slippers on. I am so worried about making sure I have the kids dressed, I on the other hand have no shoes on. I was going to go without them, but I always made fun of women who walk around all day in their pajamas and house slippers, I couldn't be a hypocrite so I ran back in the house and put on my shoes. When I dropped her off she really let the water works fly. I didn't understand it. It made me feel so helpless. I tried everything I could to cheer her up. So what did I do? I gave her hand to the teacher and left. What an awful feeling I had in my chest knowing my daughter is crying and upset and I just left her basically with a stranger. I had to do it though. It ripped out my heart. Now I have a feeling when I walk down the isle at her wedding, I might

21

punch the guy out instead of shaking his hand. When I picked her up she was as happy as a clam. She talked about what she did while at school and waived goodbye to her friends. Everything was right again. I don't know why she was sad, but I hope it doesn't happen again.

Week 6
Nov 9th-13th

Monday

My little Josie just took the biggest crap I have ever seen her take in her short existence here on earth. We fed her green beans last night and I think they multiplied while in her stomach and revolted, because her diaper could not hold the mound as it pushed its way through her diaper, through her onesie and through her shirt. Eight wipes and a new outfit later, my daughter is now cleaned up and would make any man alive proud of that dump.

What is strange about being at home with the kids and not working is I have no recollection of days or dates. I couldn't tell anyone the day of the week without stopping and thinking about it for a moment, and there is no way in hell I could even come close in knowing what the date is. When I worked, each day had a feel. Monday had a big feel, along with Friday. Wednesday had a feel, it was half-way to the weekend. But not now. Everyday has the same feel, be it Monday or Friday. Almost everyday I wake up I ask my wife what day it is. Time of day though is easy. I don't even need to carry a watch. I can tell you almost to the minute what time it is by my children's schedules of feedings and naps. Knowing the date means nothing to me since I have no where to go and no one I need to see, but the time is very important, because I am having the time of my life.

Wednesday

My wife and I had a discussion last night regarding my temper, it is very short right now. For the last couple of days I have been biting her head off at almost everything for little petty things. I have no reason to complain but my temper has got the best of me right now. I believe I figured it out. All day I feed, dress, pick-up after and do everything possible for my two daughters without a complaint in the world. But when it comes to my wife, if she doesn't put her dishes away, or pick up after herself, I jump all over her like a drill Sargent in the army. I am taking it out on her because all day my frustrations are built up from the kids. I would rather yell and vent to my wife than my children, but I need to communicate my feelings in a better way. To be honest with you, my wife has it harder than I do. I do get a break in the

23

day when my children nap. My wife goes to work all day, then comes home and spends all her time with them till bedtime. We were supposed to have a "Session" on Monday night after I got home from bowling. I walked in the door, bit her head off for not putting away the dishes, and our "Session" was cancelled. I learned something there. I would rather have a whole kitchen full of dirty dishes than have any our "sessions" cancelled. I do a real good job not losing my patience with my daughters, I rarely ever yell at them, now I must do the same with my wife, or I will have a lot of free time on my hands at night, alone.

Friday

"Friday is here since the week has past,
Where has the time gone, it doesn't last?
My children since have grown, as I have too
Everyday brings love and joy, and something new,
Six weeks so far, many more to come,
The best decision I made, was for me to stay home."

Week 7
Nov 16th-20th

Monday

Christmas. I hate it. Why? Well first of all, Christmas starts around the end of September. Most stores have their Christmas selection out before the end of September. Excuse me, isn't it four months before Christmas and Halloween and Thanksgiving come first. Another factor is the cost. You work hard all year to get yourself out of debt, then the 25th of December comes around and your burning up your credit cards buying gifts for ungrateful people you have to buy for because you know they are going to buy for you. Every year me and my wife fight about Christmas. She loves it, I hate it. It has become just a marketing holiday. You have your presents, your tree, your cards, your cloths, food, decorations, and on and on and on and on and on. I have softened a bit since now I have my own kids. Christmas is truly for kids. I have learned that. I would like it very much if I was responsible only for my own and no one else. But that will never happen. So instead of buying everything I would like to buy for my girls, I must limit myself to the things they really want, and spend our money on others. I do get excited about Christmas when December comes around, not September. I decorate the outside of our house very nicely. Every year I add some more lights and decorations. I do get caught up in it and my electric bill is well over $100 every year. We have cathedral ceiling in our house so our tree is always at least 10 feet tall. The first year in our house we bought a small tree not realizing how it would look with the ceilings and the tree seemed as big as a shrub. So since then we have to buy the biggest tree we can find. I will never own a fake tree. If you have a fake tree, while you are at it, why don't you have fake snow, fake presents and fake food. The tree will cost around $70. I have to tie the tree to the outside of the house through the window with rope so it does not fall over. (Like it did twice last year which almost killed McKenzie), then we have the Christmas cards. Every year the list seems to grow and grow along with the expense. We are anywhere from 80 to 100 cards this year. There is another $100. By the time Christmas is over, I have shopped until I am ready to kill someone. I will of had ten fights with my wife, which she will win every one on them. Spend hours in the car traveling to the relative's houses. Listen to endless Christmas songs, and go into credit card debt up to my eyeballs. With being only on one salary for the first time, this Christmas is really making me nervous. I don't want to have to eat macaroni and cheese everyday because that is all we can afford, but I want to give my kids everything possible. Christmas is for kids, and when I was a kid I loved waking up Christmas morning and seeing all the presents santa brought me. I am getting excited about shopping for my girls so they can feel what I felt when I was young waking up on Christmas day. I love Christmas.

Wednesday

When you have children you have to learn to use both arms equally well. There is no more being left-handed or right handed, you become ambidextrous. You might have a child in one arm, and be cooking with the other, when all of a sudden you feel a burning sensation in your arm as it begins to break, and you must switch arms, but still be able to accomplish the task at hand. You learn real fast how to use your opposite hand or you won't be able to do much in the time frame you have to do it in. You don't have the time to think to use your good hand when you have to act fast. If your child begins to fall down, you must grab them with whatever hand is available. You learn to feed each child and clean the dishes at the same time. It takes skill and practice, but when you are at home all day with two children at your beck and call, you become a master of being able to do eight tasks at once using both arms equally well. If you don't, your house will be a mess, you won't eat and you and your children will be naked. If God was thinking, he should have made us with four arms and four eyes because that's what it takes to raise kids.

Friday

Today was a first for me as a dad, I sat down with my oldest daughter and together we wrote a letter to Santa. I remember when I was growing up, every year I sat down with the toy catalog and wrote a detailed letter to Santa describing the toys, the model number, and what page it was on. I know now why I had to be so descriptive in my letter to Santa, but I never suspected who Santa really was.

It was very enjoyable sitting down with her to write the letter. Her list of toys consisted of one, a doll house. For the past couple of weeks she has been mentioning that all she wants for Christmas is a doll house. Not too bad right, wrong. How can I disappoint her and not have Santa get her one. Last year Santa brought her a kitchen set, and she plays with it all of the time. So my wife and I went out earlier this week to check them out and according to her, none of the doll houses in the toy stores are good enough. So she got on the phone and called a "doll house store" in which she believes they have the doll house she wants McKenzie to have. Did I mention this store is an hour and a half-away from our house and costs around $350? Well it is that far and costs that much, but you know what, on Saturday (tomorrow) I am going first thing in the morning and going to make sure Santa gets her that doll house for Christmas. When we were writing her letter, it made my heart melt knowing all she wants is a doll house and I am the one who must make sure Santa gets it for her, or her heart will be broken. I never want to break either one of my daughters hearts, ever! Even though on Christmas day when she opens her doll house and her eyes pop out of her head, Santa will get all the credit, but in my heart I know Daddy made her little girl's dream come true. That is all I want for Christmas.

Week 8
Nov 23rd-25th (Thanksgiving week)

Monday

Mission accomplished. On Saturday I got up first thing in the morning and drove to the doll house shop. I got there right when they opened. I knew going in I would buy the doll house for McKenzie no matter what the cost. Well $336.45 will buy you your daughter's first doll house. People have mentioned that girls and more expensive than boys, and I am finding that out in a hurry. Only two and half years old and this kid is already pushing me towards bankruptcy. Anyways, it is very nice. It is all wood. It has three levels and comes completely furnished. It has a mommy and a daddy, a grandma and grandpa, and a little girl and a little boy. Since McKenzie doesn't have a little brother, I asked the owner of the shop to give the little boy a sex change and turn him into a little sister. This way McKenzie can relate to her as her little sister Josie. McKenzie will be very happy, but I will be more when she walks down the stairs on Christmas morning, and the doll house is all set up for her to play with. That is all she has been talking about is getting a doll house from Santa.

Which brings me to another flash back from my childhood about Christmas. The "Santa threat." Around this time of year, I can remember whenever I was misbehaving, or wasn't listening or just being a brat, I would get the "Santa is not coming" or "you better be good if you want santa to bring you presents." This of course would always stop me in my tracks and I would instantly turn into an angel. Well I have been using this valuable piece of information on my children. I have mentioned several times when McKenzie wasn't listening that "Santa is watching" and "if you don't behave, Santa will not bring that doll house you want." It works. It works big. McKenzie totally becomes the angel she is. Yes it is cruel and mean, but hey, you only have this ace in the hole for about five weeks a year, and if you can squeeze out good behavior by threatening your children with Santa, use it.

Wednesday

The day before Thanksgiving. This year I have a lot to be thankful for. The birth of my new daughter, the Cubs making the playoffs, and the ability to stay home and raise my family. Something that people probably don't

28

realize when both parents work, then one decides to stay home, there is a huge amount of stress that disappears from your lives. The stress in our lives have been cut down dramatically. Our daycare situation was very good when we both worked. Our daycare provider was very reliable. She came to our house everyday for 18 months, and I believe she only called off maybe four times. That is pretty good. But the times she did call off without notice, we had to make a decision that morning who was going to call off work, instance stress. Everyday there was stress getting McKenzie ready in time before it was time for us to go to work. More stress making sure one of us was home on time for McKenzie when the sitter had to go home. More stress trying to get the household chores done after working all day such as cooking, cleaning, laundry, shopping etc, etc. It was very stressful trying to have a career and raise a family at the same time. Our tempers were short, and we had no energy for any bedtime fun. It wasn't much fun. If I don't get any bedtime fun after a few days, I begin to build up steam and blow like a volcano. I need to be released every so often or my pipes begin to leak.

With me being at home the last eight weeks, it has been a blessing not having to run around like chickens with our heads cut off trying to get everything done. All the chores and shopping are now done while I am at home, so at night, we actually get to enjoy each other as a family and do the things we want to do, not the things we have to do. The stress in our lives is at the lowest point it has ever been. Since I have been home, my wife is much more comfortable and relaxed at work, so while she is at the office, she can concentrate strictly on her job and not what might be happening at home. My wife is very good employee, and will go far with any company she is with. She doesn't need any outside stress added to her life, other than work related stress, since she is the sole bread winner. Without her bread, we don't eat. So I do have a lot this year to be thankful for and maybe next year I can be thankful for the Cubs winning the World Series.

Week 9
Nov 30th-Dec 4th

Monday

"Tis the season for coughs and sneezes
Fa la la la la la la la la ,
All my family members have running noses
Fa la la la la la la la la ,
Wipe them here, god bless you there,
Fa la la la la la la la la ,
When will spring time ever get here,
Fa la la la la la la la la "

For what seems to be about the last few days, all I have been doing is wiping noses. Not only the children's but mine as well. Winter has just started, so the outlook for the next five months will be, temperatures, Tylenol and tissues. The problem is if one of us gets sick, the rest of us are bound to get it. The germ gets into our house, gets inside one of us and gets them sick. Then the germ gets passed along to all the members of the house before we are able to get rid of the uninvited guest. This cycle just continues until the germ has run its course. By the time we are all healthy, I have gone through many boxes of Kleenex and various bottles of medicine. There is nothing really we can do about it. Our house is very small. It is not like we can separate the sick from the well. Even if our house was bigger, with me being the only one home, I cannot be in two rooms at the same time, unless you cut me in half, and that would hurt. So for the next five months or so, I plan on numerous visits to our family doctor, and who knows, with all my doctor visits maybe he'll invite me golfing this summer on him.

Wednesday

Misery loves company, not really. We all have become sick. McKenzie, Josie and myself, but not Lisa. She has escaped germ free as the three of us cough and sneeze in unison. All the symptoms seem to be just a cold until yesterday when McKenzie complained her ear hurt. Uh oh, ear infection. When McKenzie was six months old she got really sick. All she wanted to do was to be held, she wouldn't even eat. For three days we gave her some over the counter drugs because we thought she just had a cold. We were new parents and I am a firm believer that you don't run out to see a doctor if you nose starts to run. But after the 3rd day she began to run a temperature of over a hundred and now it was time to see the doctor. It turned out that she had a double ear infection. We felt pretty bad about not bringing her to the doctor earlier but we both agreed that as long as she wasn't running a fever, we thought she just had a cold. That was a lesson we learned as new parents, once your child starts to become sick, take them to the doctor, babies cannot tell you what is wrong with them, and I do not have a "Dr" in front of my name so I don't know either. She was on the verge of dehydration. The doctor told us to give her Pedalite. She hated it, she wouldn't drink it. So the doctor then suggested Gatorade. She loved it. She drank it like a street bum drinking a bottle of two-dollar wine. She even liked taking her medicine. To this day, she loves taking medicine and drinks a lot of Gatorade. She will probably grow up being a pharmacist or an athlete. Anyways, once McKenzie complained that her ear bothered her we all went to the doctor. The doctor checked her ear and sure enough, an ear infection. Josie's ears were fine, so the both of us have to muddle through an early winter cold. It is no fun being sick, or having to deal with sick kids, but when you mix them together, raising sick kids being sick yourself, you better have all the patience in the world, because it is absolutely the toughest situation I think I can go through right now staying at home. The best solution is to get medical attention right away so this doesn't drag on for days or weeks until you lose your sanity. I have learned that when the kids or myself even begin to have signs of being sick, we are off to the doctor's office, immediately.

Friday

The miracles of drugs have worked wonders for the Major family. McKenzie and Josie are about 90 percent healthy, I am about 95 percent. Instead of days of suffering, my decision to go to the doctor paid off and we are back to a normal household, if that is possible. We were hoping McKenzie would be better today because she has a 3rd birthday party to go to. The people in our neighborhood sort of have an unwritten rule that if your child is sick, please stay away. I agree with it, the last thing you want is another child getting your child sick. They get sick enough and don't need any help from others. McKenzie is well enough to go to the party and she is very excited. So am I. I get to spend time alone with Josie. This is the first time I actually get to spend time alone with Josie without McKenzie in our faces. When McKenzie is at school Josie sleeps, so I do not get to spend the time alone with her. I said it before and I believe the second child gets the shaft. There just isn't that enough time to bond with that child one on one, like you have with the first. It is sad in a way that you're not as attentive to the second and the quality and quantity time just isn't there like you had with the first. This is not done on purpose, it just happens. McKenzie is much more demanding than the baby. My wife and I really try to give Josie equal time. I yell at Lisa all the time that "she loves McKenzie more than Josie." It just seems Josie always gets pushed aside. Of course she doesn't, it just seems that way. She bites my head off every time I joke around with her. She doesn't think it is funny.

McKenzie went to her birthday party and I got to spend two hours alone with Josie. It was wonderful. She is such a good baby, a happy baby. What baby wouldn't be happy with me taking care of them all day? After today, I am going to try to find some other ways to get McKenzie out of the house for an hour or two a week so I can spend that time alone with Josie. She could be my last baby until grandchildren, except my daughters are not going to have sex so they are going to have to adopt.

Week 10
Dec 7th-11th

Tuesday

McKenzie cried today when I dropped her off at school. I had a feeling she was going to cry because of yesterday. Yesterday was as perfect of a day as you can get staying at home with your kids. Everything went so smooth and I was able to get a lot done around the house without even one incident. It was unbelievable how good McKenzie and Josie were. I believe they were so good because everything is beginning to take hold with Mommy being at work and me being at home.

To start, late Sunday night McKenzie was running around acting silly when she tripped and went head first into one of our kitchen chairs which is made of solid oak. She banged her head square on the forehead and began to scream and cry right away asking for "Daddy". Daddy, what about Mommy? McKenzie is asking for Daddy a lot more before Mommy. I hugged her up for about two minutes before she wanted her Mommy. It made me feel real good and real bad at the same time. Yes, I am glad she came to me to love her up, but on the same time I felt real bad for Lisa because I know she wanted to hold McKenzie and make her feel better. Lisa admitted to me later that she felt left out when McKenzie wanted her Daddy before her Mommy. McKenzie is used to me being there all day for her and when something like this occurs it is natural for her first instinct to ask for me since I am the one there most of the time for her.

Anyways, we went to the grocery store first thing. We did it with absolutely no problems. The store did not have pre-made corn bread so I had to buy a box mix to make myself. So I also decided to make homemade chicken soup. We got home and I put Josie down for her morning nap. McKenzie and I got busy making the corn bread and chicken soup. She mixed the corn bread batter with the blender and helped me bake them in the oven. She was very excited. I made the soup as she did her puzzles and played with her toy kitchen set. I was "Johnny Homemaker." Baking, cooking, cleaning, shopping everything was happening with ease. Everything I told McKenzie to do she did with no question and without whining. McKenzie can be a very bad whiner when she wants to be. It drives me nuts. The crying, the "I want my Mommy" over and over is enough for me to whip her out the window. When she gets like that I have to pause and think of all

33

the times she is a good girl for me to calm down. I don't have to think long because she is very good. Once Josie awoke from her nap we then went to mail out some presents for Christmas. The girls were perfect. We came home, we ate lunch, I cleaned up and took out all the Christmas decorations for us to put up this week. McKenzie is very excited about Christmas. The girls then took a nap and I began to decorate the house. I also managed to do this weeks ironing. I was on a roll, I couldn't stop myself. Anything I wanted to do I got done. That is why I believe McKenzie cried today. She is having a blast at home with Daddy, and with Mommy already gone to work; she just doesn't want to be without one of us. I always reassure her I will pick her up and how much fun we will have when we get back home; she then begins to feel better. To top off yesterdays perfect day, Josie is beginning to say her first words, "Da da", what a perfect day.

Thursday

I am slowly evolving into a person that I didn't know existed. I am becoming more and more domesticated as the days and weeks go by. First of all I am constantly picking up or cleaning something even when I don't have to. I could be in a restaurant or at a friends house and I have to stop myself from straightening up or just trying to help in anyway. It must be something in your brain that triggers these actions because I don't have to think about it, I just do it. After we eat at a restaurant I find myself cleaning off the table and wiping it off. In stores, if something falls of the rack or is misplaced, I find myself putting it back where it belongs. What is wrong with me? All day long I do this and now on my free time I still find myself doing domestic things outside the home. I am beginning to freak out! I need to go out and get seriously drunk. Something else I did that I wouldn't of done when I was working full time was go to an arts and craft store that just opened up last week near our house. Why did I go? No reason, just to look around. Look around for what? I am a man, not Betsy Ross. What is my problem? I should be in a sporting goods store or at a tavern. I don't know how I look myself in the mirror at night. I look at myself and try to figure out what or who I am becoming? I know in my heart the person I am is a loving father, but it makes a person think what becomes of you when you are home raising kids. It turns you into someone you never knew you could be. Not only does your life change, so do you.

Week 11
Dec 14th-18th

Wednesday

Christmas is officially out of hand. Our Christmas budget was to be $500. I believe our current tally is around $1,050. I can't help it. Being with my daughters all day knowing how good they are and how much joy they bring to my life, I want to buy them everything in sight for Christmas. I thought I hated Christmas, but something has come over me. We bought another doll house for McKenzie. Well, we didn't buy her another, we bought her a better one. I went to that new craft store by our house and they sell doll house kits. The final result when completed is a beautiful dollhouse that is nicer than my own house. The problem being it would take at least 100 hours of dedicated time to complete. I don't have that amount of time or patience to complete that task. So I asked a sales clerk if they sold the models already built that are shown on display. The answer was no. So I was completely bummed out because the doll house we bought for McKenzie seemed like a condemned building compared to these doll houses. So I stood there a few minutes thinking what I could do, and by the grace of god, I noticed there were two completely built doll houses of a same exact model. I rushed out of the store and had my wife call the manager to discuss selling us one of the houses since there were two of the same. The manger stated they usually do not sell the models, but since there were two, she would sell us the one at double the retail value of the kit. The retail value of the kit was $150, so the completed house would cost $300. I would have paid $500 if I had to. It is totally worth not having to deal with the aggravation of putting it together. To be honest, I thought $300 was ripping them off because of the hard work that has to go into assembling these houses. While I was looking at the kits, a sales clerk slipped and told me that in a week, the kits were going on sale at fifty percent off. Lisa brought up the point that they were going on sale within a week, so the manager gave us the sale price of a completely assembled dollhouse at a total cost of $150! Now I am really ashamed of myself and need to go to church and confess my sins to God, I have totally ripped off this store. Not to my attention but if they are willing to sell me this doll house at that cost, I have no alternative but to buy it, and I did. This was truly a Christmas miracle. My problem now is I have two doll houses. No problem, I will return the original one I bought. Wrong! On the receipt it states "credit only, no cash

35

refunds." I thought to myself and decided to call my credit card company up and find out if they can deny them payment if I return the dollhouse to them. The credit card company explained to me if it is posted on the receipt, they have no recourse towards the store and I must comply with them. So I thought to myself a minute, and with 2 daughters I am sure within the next year or so I will have plenty of things I can buy for them with my credit. I returned the doll house and already spent $20 of my credit the five minutes I was in the store, in which I now have $310 left.

The things you do and how you do them just amaze me when you have kids. You not only want to give them everything; you want them to have the best of everything. I love them so much that I will continue to try to give them the "best" of everything, as long a the magnetic strip on my credit card doesn't ware off. Your children always come first, whatever you need or want come second. I will have to go to church and confess my sins. My sins are loving my children to no end, and to what ends I will do for them.

Friday

Being that it is Christmas time, all week long I have been running from store to store picking up various things. It does make it harder to shop with two kids, but it is not impossible. It makes the day go by fast and they enjoy being out. I am not afraid as I take the challenge of fighting holiday shoppers. I might have my children in my arms, but my legs are free to kick. What makes me laugh is that whatever store I may be in, I can almost guarantee you that someone will come up to me and say "you really have your hands full." What does that mean? Do I come off as an inept person not being able to shop with two children? There are a lot of mothers out shopping with their kids, but nobody says anything to them. Is it because I am a man? My daughters act very good in stores as long as I don't take a lot of time. We are out and about whenever possible so my children are very adapt at going out with Daddy. I believe the more you go out with your children, the easier it gets. They become accustomed to you, as you to them. I try to get out everyday. There are days I don't make it out and by the end of the day I can be found in a corner of my house twidling my lip with my finger singing the theme song to Barney.

Week 12
Dec 21st-23rd

Monday

This is my twelfth week. I have now been home full time with my children for three full months. My first year is now one-forth over. It has gone by very fast as I watch my children grow up right in front of my eyes. I cannot recall what a typical day in the office was for me before quitting to stay home without some serious thought. I feel like I have been doing this my whole life and nothing I did before matters. This has been my destiny. My children seem very happy, I am very happy and my wife is very happy. It is four days before Christmas. This is a short week for me since my wife will be home most of the week due to the holiday. McKenzie has no school all week. This will be a good time to visit mom at work. Today was the first time I took the kids to Lisa's work. I have been very hesitant in bringing them to her work for one reason. She has three men she reports to. All three know I stay home and they tell Lisa that they think it is great, but what do they really think inside their head? I always picture this scenario in my mind. One day I bring the kids to her work, I get introduced to her boss, and as I am shaking his hand he asks me "where is your apron?" Then comes the ultimate dilemma. Do I punch him right there in the mouth, or laugh it off biting my tongue in half? I pray that the situation never arises because I really don't know what I would do. Do other men think I am a lessor man than them because I do not work? Do they think I am a wimp or a sissy? I do know this, I am a better man today raising and caring for my children than I was when I was working. If I do punch his lights out, Lisa gets fired and I get arrested. I will then have to go back to work since Lisa is out of a job. I wouldn't mind jail so much, but get a job, never! I will just have to bite my tongue, then let the air out of his tires in the parking lot when he is not looking.

As we entered the building, I immediately handed over the diaper bag for Lisa to carry. I don't know why? I am very comfortable with my situation, but this was the first time I am visiting her at work with the kids, and for some reason just didn't want to carry it. I did go out and buy a very masculine diaper bag to replace the one we had. It is a black and green backpack. It doesn't even look like a diaper bag. I am still subconscious of what people think when they see me. I am better today about it than I was three months ago, and as more time passes I won't even think twice about it. The visit went

37

fine and everyone was very nice to my daughters and I. We will visit again soon because the girls really enjoyed seeing her mother during the day, as I did.

On Wednesday of this week, I am asking my wife to express her thoughts and feelings that she may have regarding the past three months. Let's see what she has to say.

Wednesday
My wife Lisa:

I don't feel all that comfortable writing in Mark's journal but I will give it my best shot. I have benefitted the most from our decision to have one of us stay home with the girls. It was definitely one of the scariest decisions we have ever had to make. I always told Mark that it wasn't going to be a problem financially, but I was worried sick. I don't make a lot of money, but I prayed to God almost every night that somehow we would make this work out. Well, to say the least, the finances are working out just fine. Some weeks are tight, but I would eat dirt to have Mark stay home because it has been wonderful. My little girls are happier than ever. I feel so safe and secure when I leave for work in the morning. In the past, I used to sit at work and worry about McKenzie all day. I never knew what was going on when I wasn't there. I don't think anything bad ever happened between her and the nanny, but you never know for sure. Now when I leave in the morning, McKenzie gives me a big hug and kiss and says "See you after work Mom." When we had our nanny, she used to cry when I left to work, which made me drive with tears in my eyes. I never told Mark this because he would've blamed himself for not making enough money for me to stay home.
When I get home, the girls scream for me with open arms. It is the best feeling to know how much they love me. We talk about the day at dinner and the things that they did with Daddy during the day. I am amazed sometimes on how much they do during the day. He has them on the go more than I ever would I don't think a minute goes by that I don't count my blessings for my two beautiful girls and the wonderful husband that God has given me. Mark has given me more than I ever would expect from anyone. Not only is he a terrific father, but an exceptional husband. His care for the girls is so good that I don't question him anymore. I used to challenge him on feedings, sleep, etc., but not anymore. I now find myself constantly asking him what he would do in a particular situation. Wait, aren't I the mom? Sometimes it does bother me that he knows the daily routine better than me, but I need to come to terms with my role in this family. He has accepted and excelled at his role

as father, husband, and home-caretaker. Whereas, I am now the sole breadwinner. I don't mind being the breadwinner because Mark and I have always considered each of our earnings as one, I just wish I made more bread. Never did we have separate bank accounts. I just tell myself that I must do my best at work because every penny I bring home is something more I add for our family. During work I'll call just to hear Mark talk about his day and hear my girls playing happily in the background. I wasn't sure how Mark was going to handle the "Stay at home" routine, but as usual he is great. I was so worried that he was going to tell me 'forget it.' Even if he wanted to tell me that, I don't think he would because he knows how much joy and comfort he has brought to our family in the last three months. Some days he will call me at work and ask "when do you think you'll be home?" I know he really wants to tell me to get my butt home ASAP because he is losing it. That is my clue to get out of work and head home. I'll respond "On my way," and I can hear the sigh of relief in his breath. Do you know the only thing I do in the house is laundry? I can't believe it sometimes myself. Mark always has a hot meal ready when I walk in the door. He is such a good cook. I noticed that he is trying new meals now since he has more time during the day to prepare them, as opposed to running in the house after work and making something in 30 minutes. I guess what I would want everyone to know is that it isn't easy to raise children, and it isn't cheap to raise children. My husband and I have found an answer to the puzzle that works perfect for our family. Dad stays home and Mom goes to work. I wouldn't have it any other way!

Week 13
Dec 28th-Dec 31st

Monday

Christmas was very good this year. McKenzie was very excited when she woke up and noticed Santa had paid her a visit. Josie did very well opening her presents all by herself. After opening the presents she wanted to eat the wrapping paper. That kid is a good eater. Lisa did scare the daylights out of me on Christmas eve. At 10:30 pm we decided to set up McKenzie's doll house downstairs. When I wasn't looking, Lisa yelled, "McKenzie, what are you dong up?" I jumped in the air and turned around real fast to see no one. Lisa thought it was real funny. I, on the other hand, did not as I had to change my underwear. I really enjoyed playing Santa and look forward to this for many more years to come. I would have been bummed out if McKenzie found out the truth about Santa at two and a half years old.

Tuesday

Today was the first day back at work for Lisa. She was off for five days, and so was I. It was nice getting a break from the kids and Lisa enjoyed spending five full days with them. She pretty much took care of them entirely as I did other things around the house. But in the end, I think Lisa looked forward to going back to work as I looked forward to having the girls back to myself. It was nice having us all home together for that amount of time, and with New Years coming up this week, we get another long weekend togther as a family. I was a little worried the girls would miss Mommy and things would be a little harder today, but there was no crying or fussing, the beat went on.

Josie is finally holding her bottle entirely by herself. That is nice. No more standing there staring into the air while she sucks on her bottle. I am able to give it to her and walk away to do other things, very nice. Even with the five days off I was back in the groove not missing a beat. I did some ironing, went to the bank and cooked dinner all on schedule. Being at home is now in my blood and the only way you can get it out would be by a blood transfusion.

Wednesday

The new year cannot come fast enough. Today was a very bad day in more ways than one. First, Josie woke up today with a fever, a runny nose and a slight cough. We believe she is slightly sick to go along with teething. She won't even let our finger in her mouth to feel her gums. They are red and she is acting a lot like McKenzie did when cutting teeth. Josie was attached to Lisa the whole morning and cried when she left. When I attempted to put her down, she would rage before I let her go. So I held her the entire day. My patience was really tested today as a full-time parent. I can honestly say I handled it pretty well. If this happened when I started staying home I probably would have given up. It has been tough to deal with Josie when all she wants to do is be held. I explained to McKenzie that Josie needs all of Daddy's attention today and I am sorry but she will just have to watch TV or play by herself. She understood and said "Ok." In the past I would have been very frustrated and impatient, but I have learned when a child is in the need like Josie was today, nothing else matters but her and everything else has to wait. I held Josie all day until her nap and kissed her little forehead.

During all this my father calls and tells me he has bad news I automatically thought to myself that my grandma has past away. She has been living with my parents for five years now and is very old and very sick. That was not the bad news as I wish it were. My mother is going in tomorrow to have a cancerous tumor removed from her colon. My parents have known about this now for over a month and just got around to telling me. We were all just there for Christmas and everything seemed normal. My mom did seem like she lost some weight but she does go up and down with her weight so I didn't even think twice. The doctors will not know if the cancer has spread or how serious it is until they go in there and remove the tumor. Just when you think you have it bad, something like this gets slapped in your face. My sick child and me having to hold her all day seems like a walk in the park compared to the bomb my dad has just dropped on me. I have spoken to my mother and she seems to be in good spirits. She didn't want anyone to know because she didn't want anyone's New Year to be spoiled. How selfish of her but also how brave. With my mother's life hanging in the balance, you just have to sit back and think to yourself as you see your own kids grow up that you must live everyday to its fullest and enjoy every moment, because you never know what the future holds for you. Love your kids today, there may be no tomorrow. After learning the news about my mother, it just makes me more assured that I am doing the right thing by staying home raising my children. God bless her and may the new year bring good health.

Week 14
Jan 4th-8th

Monday

The new year has arrived and I will remember this new year as the worst New Year's ever of my 31 years of existence. The news on my mother was devastating. The tumor they removed along with her colon was cancerous. The cancer has also spread throughout her body. The prognosis is she would live 3 to 12 months without chemotherapy. If she agreed to chemotherapy she could extend her life longer and would have a 30 percent chance of going into remission. When I heard the news, my heart went into my stomach and I laid on the couch cradling a pillow and cried for an hour. I called my wife at work and had her come home immediately. I love my mom very much and did not expect to lose her this soon. This changes everything. From this day forward, every time I talk to her or see her it could be the last time I ever do. I have always asked the question, "Would it be better to find out someone you love is going to die, or would it be better just to get that phone call letting you know someone you love just died?" That question still cannot be answered by me. The next year is going to take a toll on my family. Death is never an easy thing, but for you to see someone dying is even worst. That is why I don't know if it is better knowing someone is going to die, or for it to just happen. There are pros and cons to both I guess. My wife's dad was 65 years old and was in Florida five years ago and he was cutting the lawn and just dropped dead of a heart attack. No warning, no "goodbyes," no "I love you's," were ever to be said again from my wife to her dad. At least I will be able to tell my mom I love her one last time before she dies. I am not going to dread on about my mother's illness throughout the journal, I wanted to mention my mother because it now puts everyday life more into perspective. The little things that I used to get upset about, or stressed over is meaningless compared to what my mother is going through. I look at my daughters and cherish every waking moment I have with them. Why? Because I love them very much and you do not know what the future has to hold for you so you do have to live for today, as I said before, tomorrow may never come. I am not going to mention my mother's condition to many friends since I do not want to be bothered with questions every time I see them like, "How is you mother doing?" or "Are you ok?" I want life to go on as normal, as I will try to treat my mother as I did before her prognosis. I believe that is what she wants. No sour faces or treating her like an invalid. Treat her like she has 30 more years to live, in which I pray every night she will.

Besides my mother's horrible news, on January second, we got hit with the second largest blizzard recorded in Chicago's history. Over twenty inches fell in one day. It was awesome. I love the snow and I love winter. The largest snowfall ever recorded was back in December of 1967. I was born in July of 1967 so I have the privilege of being alive for both record snowfalls. Another little tid-bit about the new year is during the blizzard I got a flat tire on my 4x4 pick-up truck. I have had this truck for five and half years and never had a flat or even had to change a tire, but now I did, and during a blizzard, oh how fun that was. After the blizzard and the massive dig out of snow, we are now in a deep freeze in which temperatures have reached as low as 15 below zero and a wind chill of 30 below. This new year is only four days old and it has come with a bang.

I will always remember the new year of 1999 for what it has brought me so far. With such a terrible start, I can only hope every day will bring better days and good results regarding my mother's attempt to beat cancer. I have to be positive about my mom that she will live longer than expected, but in the back of my mind I will be prepared for the worst. I believe the worst is over and the best is yet to come, maybe even a third child, only kidding.

Tuesday

McKenzie went back to school today for the first time in 2 weeks. My wife and I were a little worried she would cry when dropping her off since she hasn't been going because of the holidays, but that was not the case. In the morning we told her she was going to school today and she got very excited. I think she forgot all about school because she couldn't remember any of the names of the other kids in her class. Once we told her the names she remembered and couldn't wait to go. I couldn't wait for her to go either. I missed having the two mornings a week alone without McKenzie. Now I know why mothers always moan and groan when summer arrives and children are out of school, they are home all day. Only five out of eight children made it to class because of the bad weather. It was a good thing because McKenzie got to spend a lot of quality time with the teacher and made a lot of drawings to bring home. She calls them "her work" because her Mommy "goes to work" so she wants to be like her Mommy. It is very cute when she calls it "her work". School is also a good thing because it makes her hungry and tired. On her school days she always eats good for lunch and takes a good nap it the afternoon. My grand plan is when it is time for Josie to go the school, McKenzie should be in school full time by then, I need to find a golf course close enough to school so I can at least get nine holes in before it is time for me to pick them up. I love school.

Friday

   This week has gone by as fast as a speeding train. I cannot believe it is Friday already, and I am not complaining. The girls and I have been on the run all week catching up on chores pushed back from the holidays. Even as bad as the weather is, I will continue to get out of the house. I am not alone either. Whenever I drive out of our neighborhood, no matter how cold it is outside, or if it is snowing, I see other parents with their children getting out of the house or just standing in the driveway. You just cannot stay in the house all day, all week, locked in like a caged animal, you'll go nuts.
   Anyways, today I did they last chore on my list; get McKenzie and myself a hair cut. I was a little nervous going with Josie because I didn't know how she would act. I just can't walk out of the middle of my haircut if she starts to cry, I would have to tough it out. So McKenzie sat in the chair next to me and Josie sat on my lap. McKenzie got her haircut along with me. Josie got the worst of it though, all my clipping landed on her back and neck. The stylist had to clean us both off when she was done. All in all, it was a complete success. My fear is gone for the next time I need to get my haircut. It is getting easier and easier to do more things with the two of them. Before, when Josie was younger, I would have had some reservations on taking them out to do whatever, but not anymore. I will venture out and do almost anything now.
   Tomorrow we are all driving down to see my mom. This will be the first time I will have seen her since her operation and her diagnosis. I am a little nervous on how I will react but I am going to do my best to act like I would always act towards her. It will be hard but I must do it for my mom's sake. That is another reason why I stayed so busy this week, to keep my mind off of my mother. It really didn't work, I thought about her all the time.

Monday

The visit with my mother went pretty well. She is very upbeat and was very happy to see all of us. She is not a quitter and is going to fight this cancer to the bitter end. The house was loaded with plants and flowers. She is overwhelmed with other people's thoughts and prayers. My mom is very well liked and has a lot of friends. We all acted normal towards my mom which made me feel more comfortable being there. If I ever get sick like she is right now, I do not want anyone treating me any differently than they normally would. My mother is not denying she is sick, she knows life will go on without her, we will all prevail. She is just going to take the rest of her life that she has with us and enjoy every minute of it, and I will do the same when I am with her.

Tuesday

Over the weekend we made the transition from the infant carrier to the child car seat for Josie. She now weighs 20 pounds and the infant carrier is no longer needed. Thank God. I cannot stand the infant carrier. It is all fine for about the first 2 months when the baby only weights 8 or 9 pounds, but month after month that carrier just gets heavier and heavier and more and more awkward to carry. Whenever you try to walk with it, it bangs into your legs, you can't fit through any of your doors without banging it against the frame and you need to keep switching arms about every 15 seconds before one of your arms falls off. Our infant carrier has two clips on the back for when you put the carrier on the front of a shopping cart it will hold the baby while you push the cart. It does do that, don't get me wrong, but first of all the baby is in such an inclined position, it has a strong resemblance of the way the astronauts are positioned taking off on the space shuttle. Second thing is then trying to get the carrier off of the cart when you are done shopping is like prying nails out of wood. Add to the mix a 2-year-old in which you need to hold onto as well and you look like a juggler in a circus. Someone needs to invent one with pop-out wheels so instead of carrying it all you would need to do is push it or pull it. As young parents with McKenzie, we made the mistake once of not leaving a stroller in our van. One day Lisa and I along with McKenzie went to our mall to look for some new clothes for Lisa's ten year high school reunion. Since I forgot to put the stroller in the van, we had to carry that freaking carrier along with McKenzie from store to store for two and half-hours. It was the worst. Both our arms and biceps were sore for about a week. To this day, we have two strollers, one for the house for neighborhood walks, and one for the van for shopping and so forth. That mistake will never be made again because the stroller never ever leaves the van. Without the infant carrier, all I do now is pop both kids in to their respective car seats and off we go. I hope Lisa will let me sell the infant carrier in our next garage sale, but I doubt it. She is still grasping at straws for that third child. I keep telling you we have three children, two daughters and a dog. She doesn't believe Brodie our dog is worth mentioning, but it is. She doesn't understand having a dog is like having another child. I do everything for that dog that I do for our daughters. I take Brodie outside to potty. I feed her, take her to the doctor, wipe her butt when she has left over poop hanging from her hair, not to mention all the mounds of poop in the back I have to pick up. Plus, the damn dog follows me around all day like the kids do. I cannot get anytime to myself because I either have one, two or all three right in my tracks. So to me we have three children so if she wants another, the total will be four.

Friday

It has now snowed every day this week. All I see is white everywhere as I stare out the window wishing it was spring so I can get out of this house. The only time we get out is to the grocery store, McKenzie's school and Wal-Mart. All the other time is spent in the house and I feel like a caged animal. There is just so much you can do over, and over, and over inside the house before it gets so repetitious you want to put a bullet in your head. Just when I had enough I look up and it is nap time. The days are beginning to drag a little more now that winter is in full force, but listening to our neighbors' daycare problems still makes my staying home all worth while. Our neighbor had her baby in July of this year and went back to work in October. She brings her son to a woman's house during the day as she and her husband both need to work. Her son is always sick, he is not on a schedule, and the woman is watching far too many children for her son to get any quality attention. Our neighbor told me once she picked up her son and when she came into the house, her son was knocked over in a bouncy chair with dried up snots all over his face. She doesn't know how long his nose been running on his face or how long he laid on the floor before she got there. I am sure there are many other incidents like that we don't even know about. That is why I am blessed that I am able to stay home and care for my children. I fully understand why people have to put their children in daycare because of the world we live in. It is just too expensive to be able to live the life you want for yourself and children sometimes with only one income. Most families need two incomes now a days to just make it. But there are some people who put there children in daycare and want to work when they really don't have to. That bothers me a lot. There is one thing needing to work, but wanting to work so you can keep up with the Jones' makes me ill. Lisa knows a few people at her work that have children in daycare, and when they take a day off still bring there child to daycare so they can have the day alone. You want to be alone, don't have kids. I understand completely that you need time by yourself but bring your child to grandma's house or to a friend's house for a few hours. Don't let a daycare raise your child, take responsibility for what is yours, your children. There is a time and place for you and your spouse to spend quality time alone, and putting you children in daycare to do it is not the answer. My wife and I have given up so much for our children and I wouldn't have it any other way. We will raise and care for our children, not society. If that means I don't buy a new car every couple of year's so be it. If I don't have the latest fashions in clothing, so what. We have to watch every penny, but I get to watch every hair grow on their head, and watch every step they make. We might not be able to afford to buy or do the things we used to when we had two incomes, but the last time I checked, love is free.

Tuesday

I am teaching McKenzie the meaning of winning and losing. I believe it is important to teach children how to win and how to lose. We each grab a puzzle and race to finish it. She really enjoys it and really gets into it. Throughout the whole time she is doing her puzzle she yells "I'm gonna win" and eight out of ten times I let her. The times I do beat her she just smiles and says "I lost, you win" and is very cute in doing so. Children need to learn how to win and lose gracefully. I do not want her growing up to be a spoiled winner or poor loser. A few months ago there was a debate on the radio that a suburb in Chicago has a soccer league that doesn't keep score because they don't want children to feel the disappointment if they lose. I believe that theory is complete garbage. Children have to feel the glory of winning and as bad as it may sound, the sorrow of losing. Why? A child must feel the satisfaction of winning. They must be taught to win gracefully, but winning something such as a sports event or a spelling bee contest provides them with hard work and dedication, they can become the best at whatever and be rewarded for it. It also goes the other way when you lose. Your child will not always be the best and will lose more times than win, and they must be taught how to deal with the pain and how to overcome it. Winning and losing just doesn't happen in sporting events, it happens in everyday life. A good example is applying for that first job when you are an adult. It may take you five or ten or twenty interviews before you land yourself a job. Winning and losing is a big fact of life. I can very easily let McKenzie win every time, but I don't want her to think she cannot lose. No matter how good you may be, there is someone out there better than you, and someone else out there better than him or her. There will be plenty of times in McKenzie's life she will lose, but as long as she tried her best and feels good about it, she will always be a winner to me.

Thursday

Josie is a little con artist. For a few weeks now I have been complaining to Lisa that Josie is lazy because she hasn't begun to crawl yet. According to the bible of parenting *What to Expect the First Year*, there is no clear cut date when a baby should begin to crawl. It is not a stepping stone they consider in a baby's development. Some babies don't even crawl; they just cut out that step and begin to walk. That is what we thought was going to happen with Josie. Whenever we would set Josie down on the floor she would play nice, but as soon as she landed on her stomach, she would have nothing to do with it and would just rage tears until one of us picked her up. Well, she had us both fooled. She couldn't keep her little secret anymore. Last night Lisa, McKenzie and Josie were on the floor playing when all of a sudden Josie took off crawling across the floor like if her pants were on fire. She sprinted across the rug to grab at one of the toys that McKenzie was playing with. This was a first; she never even attempted to crawl before last night. She must have been practicing in her crib at night because she crawled like a turtle chasing a mouse. We were both in complete shock. My little baby Josie has been playing her Mommy and Daddy like fools getting us to pick her up every time she cried on her stomach when the whole time she could crawl. Unbelievable! I have to hand it to her though; she kept her secret as long she could before she had to break it going after that toy. If a nine-month-old baby can manipulate me like that, I am really going to have my hand full when these two grow up. I already foresee me trying to punish them for something they did wrong, all they will need to do is cry and bat their big blue eyes at me, and I am sure I will crumble into a helpless jellyfish. I wish they didn't have to grow up so fast, but no matter how big they get, they will always be my babies.

Monday

Lisa's mom came over today to spend the day with the girls. It would have been awesome if the weather was in the 70's so I could of went golfing. But there aren't many days in the 70's in the month of January when you live in Chicago. She stayed until the girls went down for a nap. They loved seeing and being with her, and grandma was ready for a nap too by the time she left to go home. The day dragged for me though. Since grandma was playing and feeding the girls, I really didn't have much to do. I made lunch and cleaned up but besides that, I basically just sat there and watched the clock. It was nice to have contact with another adult, but I did miss being with my girls alone. I welcome anyone to visit me during the day, especially if you're over the age of 18.

We have a big decision to make in the very near future. Yesterday, Lisa received a call from a former boss of her's at work and offered her a job in Atlanta. They want her to start April 1st of this year. The salary is good, they will pay for all our moving expenses and the opportunity for financial security with this new company is very positive. It really is a no-brainer. With us on one income, we have to look at every opportunity that arises to better suit our family. With the cost of living so much cheaper in Atlanta, we would be able to provide the girls a lot more than we can living in the Chicago area. We both have lived in Illinois all our life, and we both are ready to move and see what else is out there. I called a good friend of mine, the one I go golfing with every weekend in the summer, and told him to pack his bags we are moving to Atlanta. He is 33 years old, divorced with no kids, therefore, it would be easy for him to relocate with us. He has no reason to stay here and all the reason to move with us. Yes that is right, golf 360 days a year! He is packed and ready to go. The feeling and timing is right for us to make this move. Even with my mother as sick as she is, she wants us to do what is right for us and no one else but us. So the next few weeks will be very busy for "Super dad." Not only will I have the duty of raising my two daughters, but I will also have to sell our house and buy a new house 700 miles away. The only thing is we can't move until bowling season is over. In six years I have missed bowling once, and that was when I went on a cruise. I am not a geek, I am dedicated.

Wednesday

When it was time to tell my mother that I was quitting my job to stay home full-time with the girls, I was a little nervous. For the past two years I was hinting towards the idea with her to feel her out and she was luke-warm to the idea at best. She would always say "You won't be happy," or, "Why would you want to do that?" Of course there are thousands of reasons why I wanted to stay home, but still she is my mother and I just didn't want to upset her. So when it came time to tell her I was quitting to stay home, I had a prepared speech of why it is going to be so beneficial for me to do so. One of the many positives I mentioned was that she would see me and the girls more because I can visit her during the week and not have to wait for a holiday or the weekends. Today was the first time since October I have decided to venture down to see my mom without Lisa, and let's just say the day was a disaster. Why? Josie cried like someone was cutting her leg off with a dull knife for three straight hours. It was horrible. I felt so bad for my mom because she looks forward to seeing her grandchildren, and for one of them to cry and scream the whole time couldn't of made her feel any better. She thinks Josie was teething because her gums were very white and wanted to chew on everything she could put into her mouth. That might be the case, but the only way she would stop crying was for me to hold her. It got old, very old, and very fast. If my mom didn't live 70 miles away I would of went home right away. We made the trip so I wanted to stay a few hours. It got so bad, I called Lisa at work and told her she might have to come home early because I am ready to hang myself from Josie's crying. She said she will come home ASAP or for me to page her if I need her to come home any sooner. That was very comforting as I stayed as long as I could before I couldn't take it anymore. I had to cut my visit short with my mom. The visit was almost three hours and even though Josie cried the whole time, my mother appreciated our visit very much. I felt bad but good at same time. Here is the kicker. I was able to get home fast enough for Josie to sleep another hour before Lisa would be home to relieve me. It was 5:30 pm and no Lisa. Josie has already eaten her dinner and I haven't started ours. Josie is quiet and seems to be doing a lot better. I really need her mother to be home to help out because I am behind in getting dinner ready and I could not afford Josie to blow another gasket. The phone rings and it is Lisa asking me if she needs me home right away. She states there are a few things she would like to finish up first before heading home. What? Is she an idiot or is she suffering from Alzheimer's Disease? I distinctly remember telling her on the phone I need her home right away because Josie was having a difficult day.

She promised me she would! Now she is on the phone oblivious to our previous conversation earlier that day so I just went nuts on her. I snapped as I screamed and whipped the phone to the floor. Just when I did, Josie decided to deposit her dinner in her diaper and I needed to change it. When I was changing her diaper the phone rang. I knew who it was, Lisa. I didn't want to answer it because I couldn't stand to hear her excuse of being insensitive and unwilling to be with her child in need. She left a message on the answering machine stating she was wrong and forgot what a horrible day it was today and is on her way home. I finished dinner so I calmed down by the time Lisa got home. I wanted to be too busy eating to yell at her. I know she has a lot of pressure and is very busy at work. I am as supportive as I can be, but when I need her to be home, I need her home. There hasn't been a time yet that she had to call off work to stay home with our daughters. I know my responsibility is the girls and hers is her job, but when I need Lisa, or Lisa needs me, everything else must wait, family comes first.

Thursday

Last night Lisa received a call from the company in Atlanta wanting to interview her on February 12th. So with that in mind I had to get busy and busy I was. It went a little like this:

6:30 am woke up
6:30 - 7 took a shower and got dressed
7 - 7:30 ate breakfast, read the paper and made a deposit
7:30 - 8:30 did the weeks ironing
8:30 - 8:45 drove McKenzie to school
8:45 - 9:00 drove back from school
9 - 9:15 rocked Josie to sleep for her morning nap
9:15 - 10:30 met with a real estate agent regarding the sale of our house
10:30 - 10:45 woke Josie up and fed her a bottle
10:45 - 11 drove to McKenzie's school to pick her up
11 - 11:15 went to the bank to pay van payment for the month
11:15 - 11:30 drove home and picked up the dry cleaning on the way
11:30 am - 12 pm fed Josie her lunch and gave McKenzie a small snack
12 - 12:30 called various airlines to book two tickets to Atlanta
12:30 - 12:45 reserved a car rental
12:45 - 1 prepared McKenzie's lunch and gave Josie her snack
1 - 1:15 ate lunch
1:15 - 1:30 began to give Josie her afternoon bottle
1:30 - 1:45 played with Josie and McKenzie before afternoon naps

1:45 - 2 put McKenzie down for her afternoon nap

2 - 2:15 changed Josie's diaper, gave her the rest of her bottle, put her down for her afternoon nap

2:15 - 2:45 did the dishes, picked up around the house

2:45 - 3 called the realtor in Atlanta to set up meeting for February 12th

3 - 4:00 sorted through all the bills, paid the bills, and balanced the check book

4 - 4:30 worked on my journal

4:30 - 4:45 woke McKenzie up and gave her afternoon snack

4:45 - 5:00 woke Josie up and changed her diaper and prepared her dinner

5 - 5:30 fed Josie her bottle and two jars of food for dinner

5:30 - 6:00 prepared our dinner

6 - 6:30 ate dinner

6:30 - 7 cleaned up from dinner

7 - 7:30 helped Lisa give McKenzie and Josie their baths

7:30 - 8:00 played with Josie and McKenzie along with Lisa

8 - 8:30 exercised

8:30 - 8:45 helped Lisa with Josie and McKenzie to get them ready for bed

8:45-9 took a shower

9-9:30 laid on couch with a bowl of ice cream and watched a re-run of *News Radio*

9:30pm went to bed!

I didn't have time to blink today otherwise I would have missed something. I have a feeling the next few weeks will be very similar to the one I just experienced. I will need a lot of patience from myself and a lot of cooperation from my daughters. Everything should work out; otherwise I will have a nervous breakdown by the time this move (if we move) is over.

Week 18
February 1st-5th

Tuesday

All day I feel like I am a referee in a boxing match for the heavy weight championship of the world. I am constantly yelling at McKenzie for bothering Josie. Now that Josie is able to crawl around the house and play by herself, McKenzie isn't in the sharing mood. She was really good when Josie was smaller about sharing her things, but now that Josie is actually able to pick her toys up and play with them, McKenzie isn't willing to share without us reminding her to do so. In my sleep I hear myself yelling, "stop it," and "McKenzie, quit it" or "knock it off." Whenever Josie is playing with something and is enjoying herself, McKenzie comes over and rips it out of her hands. Josie cries or fusses and I am there to correct McKenzie every time. This little episode happens about twenty times a day. McKenzie will also wrestle with her until she begins to cry. That is probably my fault because I wrestle all the time with McKenzie and I often don't let up until she begins to cry. Lisa yells at me for doing so but my response is I am trying to toughen her up. Now I have McKenzie beating on Josie and Lisa getting upset with me when they do so. I let them go at it until Josie begins to cry. I do so because I believe in some way Josie does enjoy it and they need to learn how to play together. McKenzie may be getting the better of Josie right now, but Josie only weighs eight pounds less then McKenzie does, so when Josie is able to walk, there are going to be many good rounds of knock-down fighting between the two of them. That's when I am really going to have to act like a referee and put them both in the corner until the bell rings for them to come out fighting. I think it will be fun to watch, but Lisa doesn't agree.

So we are working with McKenzie about how to share and get along with her sister. McKenzie loves her sister very much, it is not a "hate" thing at all, but Josie gets a lot more attention now that she is able to crawl and is learning how to walk. Lisa spends more time with Josie when she comes home from work so McKenzie is just trying to find ways to get our attention. As the old saying goes, "any attention, good or bad, is better than no attention at all."

54

Thursday

I have been feeling a little self-conscious lately of the intake of television McKenzie watches during the week. I don't know why I am so concerned, but I am. I am caught up in all the hype how television is a "vast wasteland" and children should be doing other things besides watching television. There are some mothers I hear saying how their children never watch TV, but I know that is a bunch a bull because their children sure can identify characters that are only shown on TV. It is too hard right now for McKenzie to do much of anything since we are in the dead of winter. When I first started staying home, we were outside a lot and TV wasn't even a factor. Since we are unable to hang outside, television just needs to take its place. A comforting feeling is that she does go to school twice a week for two and a half hours per day. I did not go to any preschool when I was growing up. Everyday for at least an hour we do get out to such places as the grocery store or Wal-Mart so she isn't planted in front of the tube all day. The programs she watches are all on public televison and all have learning skills attached to them. She is only 32 months old and she is very bright. She knows her ABC's, can count to 20, knows all her colors, can spell her name (McKenzie, not very easy) and can operate the computer almost as well as I can. I know for a fact when I was her age I didn't even talk in complete sentences. I was the third child so whatever I wanted I just pointed and my brother and sister gave it to me so I wouldn't cry. Many people have mentioned they believe McKenzie is gifted. I do not have anything to base it on so I just take the comments with a grain of salt. Once spring is here, or we do decide to move to Atlanta where there is warmer weather, we will be outside doing a lot more things than watching televison. So for now, I will let the television occupy her for the most part, but I do have time blocked out during the day when she doesn't watch TV and she must color, do her puzzles or play on the computer. If she is gifted and turns out to be a very smart person, I do want some credit.

Baby invention:
The automatic bath tub.
It acts like a dishwasher but is safe to put your children in.
Place them in, turn it on and in two minutes they are cleaned, dried and spotless.

We give our children baths three times a week. The whole process takes about a half-hour. After a long hard day, giving the children a bath is not the most pleasurable experience, but it needs to get done. I would buy the "baby bather," someone just needs to invent it.

In the summer, when I played softball I would usually take a shower afterwards. If I got home early enough, I used to take McKenzie in the shower with me in place of her bath. She loved it and wanted to take showers all the time. Maybe I will try to give them showers once in awhile in place of the baths.

Friday

It's official; our house is up for sale. Last night the realtor came over and we signed the contract to put our house on the market. Does Lisa have the job in Atlanta? We don't know. Do we like Atlanta? We don't know. We won't know the answers to these questions until a week from now, but we are 99 percent sure we will be relocating down to Atlanta. I hope so because someone is already coming to look at our house tonight. What are the odds that someone will offer to buy our house the first day it is on the market? We don't even have any place to move. The odds of that happening are slim, but if the offer is good and we accept it, I kept some old boxes that should accommodate four relatively nicely. It is sad to see the for sale sign go up in front of our house. We put our souls into this house and this is the house that we brought our two lovely daughters home to from the hospital. It will be very sad to move, losing friends, moving farther away from our families, new surroundings, different ways of living and much much more. However, I look at it this way; it is a sad old ending to a great new beginning.

Week 19
February 8th-12th

Monday

Teething for Josie has not been easy on her. She has one tooth now and more are on the verge of popping through. She constantly runs a fever, pulls her ears, doesn't want to drink her bottle and has the runniest, smelliest diapers that would make Freddy Kruger run away scared. McKenzie took teething very well when she was a baby. A few times she would run a fever, but teething overall never bothered McKenzie the way it has affected Josie. One time, McKenzie had four molars come in at once and she didn't even flinch about it. Josie is a better eater and sleeper than McKenzie was, but McKenzie was walking at 10 months and Josie is still a couple months away. It just proves that every child is different and you never know what to expect from child to child in their respective stages of life.

Josie is progressing very well and she is beginning to evolve into a human being more and more each day. She is able to pull herself up on the furniture and walk. She had the big move the other day; going from the couch and reaching out and turning onto the coffee table. It is funny watching the terrified look in her eyes as she is just about to let go of the couch and grab onto the coffee table. Once the ordeal is over, I clap very loud and her face lights up like she just won the lottery. Of course McKenzie, the green-eyed jealous monster has to show off she can do it also. I humor her and clap for her as well, but Josie is the one I am proud of at this moment. Josie has also learned to wave, say the words; mamma, bye bye and I believe night night, but I am not sure. She is growing into her own personality very nicely and as soon as she is able to walk and talk completely, I will be her devoted personal servant as I am already for McKenzie.

Tuesday

When I decided to stay home and raise my daughters, my wardrobe drastically changed. I went from having to wear a shirt and tie at the office to wearing sweat pants and a sweatshirt at home. There are many kinds of dress codes when you work such as "Business wear" and "business casual." Business wear may consist of a suit, and business casual a shirt and tie. My line of clothing is called "parent wear." You don't need to "dress for success" or wear expensive clothing when staying home. All week you get spit up on, spilled on, urinated on and so forth. Its like you're an athlete, when you begin the game you're nice and clean, but when the game is over, your filthy and you need a shower. No need to spend too much on cloths, just buy durable clothing that can handle many washings. Being comfortable is also a must. You're constantly bending, kneeling, crawling, etc., so wearing tight jeans to show off your figure is not a priority. I wear the same clothes Monday through Friday. I change my underwear, socks and t-shirt daily, but my sweat pants and sweatshirt remain the same. On the weekends I do wear nicer cloths for two reasons. I want to look good for my wife since I don't see her much during the week hoping to score, and after wearing sweats all week, I don't want to turn into a total bum. We save a lot of money on dry cleaning and saves my wife time with the laundry and me on ironing. Someone in the fashion world needs to come up with a line of clothing suitable for stay home parents. All of these characteristics must be included; they must be comfortable, stylish, inexpensive, durable and waterproof. Calvin Klein must be notified at once.

Thursday

It is gut check time. Our house did not sell in one day, it sold in five! I cannot believe our house is sold and we have not made the final decision that we are going to move. The house is sold for the exact amount I wanted, and the couple buying the house is very nice. Problem being is Lisa has not accepted the job in Atlanta since no job in Atlanta has been offered to Lisa. Lisa is completely freaking out! So I talked to a lawyer and he told me to write a contingency clause into the contract that says, "This contract is contingent on the Major's moving to Atlanta on or by February 15th." This way if we to decide to back out of the sale, there will be no legal recourse against us. That has made Lisa a little more secure, because her greatest fear, which is mine too, is that Lisa and I are not satisfied with the offer and decide not to move and we just sold our house for no good reason. We are though 99.999999 percent we will be moving and that is why we put our house up for sale so soon. The realtor told us the average is 45-60 days. I would say 5 days is off his chart. We fly out tomorrow at 6 am. Lisa has interviews all afternoon as I will be with a realtor scoping out the greater Atlanta area. I told Lisa this morning that I am 100 percent behind her on her decision. If she wants the job and wants to move to Atlanta, I am 100 percent with her. If she decides the job is not for her and doesn't want to move, I am still 100 percent with her.

No matter what the outcome is, it will be nice to get away for a couple of days alone with my wife. No kids, no work, no diapers, no Barney, just us. All your life you can't wait to have children and it is the best day of your life when you actually get to hold your own flesh and blood after birth. Then there is the second best day in your life, the day you get to leave the kids with grandma and spend a weekend in a hotel alone with you wife. I am packed and ready to go, if you know what I mean.

My mother started chemotherapy this week. I called her Monday night to wish her luck and tell her I love her and that I am always thinking of her. I wanted to talk to her before her first dose because I didn't know how she was going to react towards the treatment. On Tuesday night she called me and was doing fine. I joked around with her and asked her if her head was glowing green and she laughed. She was in good spirts and told me she is just taking it "day by day." If you think about it, we all are taking it "Day by day" and you don't know what the day may bring. I thought of not moving because of my mother's condition but she would be very upset. I don't want to get her upset; I want her well more than words can express. Lisa and I have to do what is right for our family, and if moving to Atlanta will give a better quality of life for the girls and us then we must take that chance. Life moves pretty fast, opportunities come along only once in awhile, if any at all. If you don't stop and look around at your life, you might miss it.

Monday

Does the baby need a diaper change? That is the question many ask themselves, and there are various techniques in answering that question. Some will open the diaper and look for little treasures. Others such as myself will lift the baby and stick their nose on the babies butt and take a whiff like two strange dogs meeting for the first time. Some will stick their fingers between the baby's leg and the diaper to peak inside. Anyway you look at it, it is something we all do, but do not like to talk about. I remember when I didn't have children, changing a dirty diaper was one of the things in life I swore I would never do. Now I do it six times a day. It is different when you have your own child. The poop just doesn't seem as gross as someone else's poop. It is not like your child's poop doesn't stink, because it does, it is just you love your child, and whatever comes out. Changing Josie's diaper has become a bigger chore than in the past. I used to be in and out within a minute, but not anymore. She turns, twists, wiggles, kicks and bends every time I try to change her. I grab her by both her feet with one hand, and with the other try to wipe her, lube her, and put on a new diaper. By the time I am done I feel like a rodeo cowboy trying to lasso a calf. I don't know how some parents keep their children in diapers until they are three or four years old. McKenzie was trained in eighteen months and Josie will be right behind her. I just cannot imagine changing a three or four-year-old's diaper. McKenzie is a few months away from being three. There are times that her poop in the toilet is as big as mine. Then I think to myself that her poop, instead of being in the toilet where it belongs, it can be smashed in a diaper and I would have to wipe and scrap it off her butt. I would not enjoy that at the least. People say differently about training their children at early ages. The experts say not to train your children until they are interested and are ready. I think the only way to get them ready and interested in going on the toilet is to get them to do it. I can only think of positives in getting your children trained as soon as possible, no negatives. The cost of diapers alone was my biggest motivator. I don't know, everyone is different and has their own opinions and ideas, but my wife and I both agree, the sooner the better.

The update on our move is that it is a go. Lisa loves the opportunity she is going to have with the new company and we like the area of which we will move to. I spent all day Friday looking at different areas and on Saturday, Lisa and I both spent the day looking at new housing. We are very excited and can't wait to start our new life in Atlanta. The opportunity is too good to pass up and our families are behind us all the way. It will be hard to leave, but I am confident we will see our families the same if not more than we do now. We didn't find a house we both agreed on to buy, so in 2 weeks Lisa and I are going down again for three days and hopefully find ourselves a house we both like. If we don't, we will have to sleep in our van. Life will be a lot different down there as compared to now. We both agree 100 percent this is the right time and the right place to move. A wise man once said, "The only thing constant is change."

Thursday

People who haven't seen me since I have decided to stay home have new views on me. I have recently visited our dentist, who is a mother of three, and visited some of Lisa's old college roommates. They have all told Lisa the same about me; I am much more relaxed and seem very happy and content. Lisa has mentioned to me before that people have told her that I am a different person. In a way it is a compliment, and in another way I take offense. What was I before a mean old man or something? People also state the staying home must agree with me because I seem much more at peace than I did before when I was working. I must have been some sort or walking time bomb before this, but I really didn't notice. It is hard to notice something unless you look from afar, especially something about yourself. Staying home has agreed with me and I am much more content and happy than when I worked. It was destiny. My stress level is practically zero. I have no more traffic to deal with, no more road rage. No more waking up and stressing out about work, or how am I going to cut the lawn, cook dinner and take care of the girls all after work. I don't have to worry about that anymore since now I am home all day to get things done. I used to be short tempered and fly off the handle anytime something didn't work out or go my way. Not anymore. My patience level is very high and I take things in stride much better. I have noticed that myself. It takes a lot more than spilt milk to make my head explode. The chores I used to hate doing I love to do now because I get to do them with my daughters. McKenzie loves to help, sometimes too much, but all in all she is becoming a great help around the house. I hear it all the time from my male friends telling me, "I don't know how you can stay home all day with the kids, fifteen minutes alone with them and I want to kill them". I really don't say anything back, I mainly just smile and nod my head in agreement. But what I am really thinking is I don't know how you can work all day locked up in a cubicle, then risk your life in traffic day after day, year after year, while your children are at home growing up and you're not around to see it. My smile is for my happiness and my nodding is letting them know they are all fools.

Week 21
February 22nd-26th

Monday

I have officially taken over another household chore and two-thirds of another. I am now responsible for paying the weekly bills. I have decided to lesson my wife's load once again to help her spend more time with the girls, and more importantly more time with me at night. It takes anywhere from a half an hour to an hour to do our weekly bills, so that is that much more time Lisa has to spend with her family during the week. I have also decided to give the girls their baths on Tuesday's and Thursday's during the day. This just leaves Lisa giving them their baths on Sunday's only. Once again, more quality time for her during the week to spend time with her family instead of doing chores. So it comes down to this; the only household responsibility that Lisa has claim to is the laundry, that is it. I am in full control of everything else that happens in this house. I accept the challenge. I would have to think it is very normal for the home caretaker to have full control of everything that happens within the home. I am home all day and if I want things to run the way I want them to run, who else to trust to make sure that happens than myself. Not that I don't trust Lisa, but I have accepted that her main responsibly is her career and for her to be able to support us financially, and mine to support her by taking care of our daughters and everything else that goes with staying at home. I like having this responsibility because I will not have anyone else to blame but myself if something goes wrong, but whom am I kidding, nothing can go wrong with me in charge.

We fly out on Thursday to Atlanta once again to try and find a house. The pressure to buy a house is beginning to mount as Lisa's new company wants her to start in April. It would be no problem moving into an apartment for a few months if it weren't for the girls. I don't want them cooped up in a cramped apartment, especially in the summer, when they should be outside playing and enjoying themselves. We keep telling McKenzie when we move she will have a pool and a park to go to everyday, she is very excited and so am I. I will enjoy this summer very much as I am ready for my first summer without having to work since I graduated from college. Sure I have two girls to take care of, but instead of being chained down inside a cubicle finding out what the company's net profit was for the month, I will be pool side with a beer and I diaper bag. Lets's think for a moment, cubicle or pool side, which sounds better?

Wednesday

Today was haircut day once again for McKenzie and me. Last time we both got our haircuts I had Josie sit on my lap the whole time while the stylist cut my hair. I was a little smarter this time. The haircut place is inside a grocery store so instead of Josie sitting on my lap collecting all of my clippings on her back, I put her inside a grocery cart and pulled the cart as close as possible next to me as the stylist cut my hair. Josie just sat there in amazement as McKenzie sat in the chair on the other side of me waiting patiently for her turn. The stylist, who was an elderly lady, did mention my children were very well behaved, unlike some others she has experienced being very unruly. I do have good children, but I wouldn't expect anything less with me in charge all day. Which brings me to a comment the stylist made when I first walked in and asked for a haircut. She asked me if I was babysitting today. I told her I am home everyday and people don't babysit their own children, they raise them. Why do people always assume since I am with two small children I am babysitting? I also still hear a lot of times, "Boy, you have your hands full." I don't even acknowledge that comment anymore, I pretend I don't hear them. Our haircuts turned out fine and I tipped the stylist anyways, even though I didn't like her comment about me babysitting. She did however tell me my children were very well behaved, which was nice, and I do feel sorry for her, unlike me, she has to work!

Thursday

Today was a very busy day as I prepared for our house hunting trip in Atlanta. I cooked meals for grandma, packed our suitcase and made sure everything is in order for when we are gone. McKenzie is very excited that grandma is coming again for a few days, but doesn't want us to leave either. The last time we went, she often asked grandma where we were. It breaks my wife's heart when we have to leave the children behind, but it is necessary for us to do so. It is easier for me to leave without them since I am home all day, but Lisa has a hard time. Before we had the girls, Lisa used to bawl her eyes out when we would go away for the weekend and we would drop Brodie off at the kennel. So if she had a hard time with Brodie, I am sure it is extremely hard with the girls. Hopefully we find a house this weekend and we don't have to go down again without all of us going as a family. We are all very excited about starting our new life together in Atlanta.

Week 22
March 1st- 5th

Monday

I have said before that I am an antagonist, but my fun with McKenzie is running out. I used to really be able to tease her, but she has learned the difference of when I am kidding around with her and when I am serious. I taught her by the phrase, "Are you pulling my leg?" So before when I used to tease her by telling her she can't take a nap, or she can't watch a Barney tape, she would cry and be very sad. Why it made me laugh watching my own child cry, I don't know maybe it was the power I had over her. Now when I try the same stunts, she will look at me and ask me, "Are you pulling my leg?" then I will just smile and tell her "yes." McKenzie will do the same to me. She will tell me "Daddy I am sad" and I will ask her "what is wrong" and she will respond "im pulling your leg". It is good that she has learned the difference between teasing and when someone is serious. It will come in handy when she goes to school and when some kids are making fun of her for who knows what (kids can be pretty mean sometimes) and instead of crying and getting upset about it, she can walk away knowing in her head they are just messing around with her. Or I can teach her karate and have her just kick the crap out of the kids that make fun of her, but we will try this approach first. I only have Josie left to torment from here on out. I do torment Lisa, and she gets very annoyed with me when I do, but then I have the threat of being cut off and I don't want to be in that situation. I have the dog, but Brodie is getting too old, she just walks away and hides when I mess with her. I don't know, I might have to have more children so I can get my power back and be the antagonist I enjoy being.

It is official, we are moving to Atlanta and there is no turning back. This past weekend Lisa and I bought a house and are very excited about our new future together. It is a gorgeous house with plenty of room in a subdivision that I hope the girls can make numerous friends. There is a park, a pool and tennis courts the home owners can use during the year. The next month is going to be very busy for Lisa and I. It is hard enough raising two small children, but then having to move while doing so is going to be a very large and tiring task. I have made several phone calls already today trying to get this move going and I haven't even scratched the surface. It is going to take a lot of patience for Lisa and I to get through the next several weeks, but once we are down in Atlanta and we are all moved in, it will be worth the sweat and blood that were about to occur.

Wednesday

I have been doing a lot of fishing lately, not the type of fishing which most people are all-familiar with. There is no lake, there is no pole and there are no fish. The type of fishing I have been doing is "booger fishing." With the weather being cold outside and it being so dry in the house, the girls get these big green dried up boogers lodged up in their noses and have no way of blowing them out. So this is where I come into play. I put them on their backs, I look inside for the booger and very gently insert a pair of tweezers inside their nostrils. I am very careful to make sure I do not touch the inside of their nostril or clamp onto anything else but the booger. It is very similar to the game of operation, in which you need to pretend you are operating on somebody and if you instrument touches the body a buzzer goes off. I like to think of it as fishing, you go in not knowing what to expect to pull out, and once you have a grab of it you don't want to let it go because you don't know if you are able to get it back. Once I am successful in fishing the booger out of either of their noses, I show them the booger and they are very proud. Call me a freak, but I enjoy booger fishing.

Friday

Today started off as any other Friday. After Lisa went off to work, the girls and I went to Wal-Mart for our weekly supplies. After Wal-Mart, Josie went down for her morning nap and McKenzie watched some television. I made some phone calls regarding our new house in Atlanta. Around 10 a.m. McKenzie told me she didn't feel good and had a headache. I took her temperature and it turned out she had a fever of 101. McKenzie is very rarely sick, so when she says she doesn't feel good I believe her. So I told her to go on the couch and rest. Around 10:30 am she threw up all over herself, the couch, her baby doll and blanket. It was ugly. I don't mind the smell of pooh, or skunk, or feet, but throw up really gets to me bad. Several times when I was trying to clean it up, I had to step back and get fresh air because I began to gag. Even though it was my own child's throw up (which should make it easier to clean up since it is my own daughter's) I had a very difficult time in doing so. I did however manage to clean her up and everything else. I will be smelling that smell for weeks, it just gets under my skin and won't go away. I called Lisa and told her what has taken place. Her response was to take her to the doctor. I am not one to jump to the doctor every time my child sneezes or coughs, so I wanted to wait to see how she was going to feel after awhile. Lisa was not to happy that I was going to wait because of the strep epidemic that has plagued the Chicago land area as of late. Eleven people have died in the past month due to type A strep. It is very scary. I looked in her throat and it looked normal so I just wanted to play it by ear. She told me she felt a lot better and wanted to take a little catnap. She did and woke up hungry. I fed her some cantaloupe and woke Josie up from her nap. After I fed Josie, I wanted to run out to a store so I asked McKenzie how she felt. She told me she had a headache and her throat hurt. That was it, I called the doctor immediately. Once she told me her throat hurt her I wasn't messing around and wanted a doctor to see her now. I told the office I would be there in 5 minutes. All three of us arrived at the office as we waited patiently. The office just got an upgraded computer system so they wanted me to fill out all the registration forms we had to fill out with our first initial visit. I explained as calmly as I could to the nurse that I will not be filling out any forms at this time. I have a very sick child hanging on one arm, and a 10-month-old hanging on the other, and they want me to fill out countless forms. I don't think so. I told them I would take everything home with me and fill it out later and return it to them tomorrow. They backed away and said ok. Forty-five minutes passed by when McKenzie got up from her chair, let out a belch and threw up all over the waiting room carpet. I jumped up and ran to the nurses window and screamed for the doctor as my daughter has now thrown up twice within two hours. A very nice lady who was waiting to see the doctor also, helped McKenzie clean up and gave her a drink of water. My nerves at this point are shot. I am not at all concerned of the mess McKenzie made; I just want to see a doctor now. The doctor heard my yelling and grabbed McKenzie and went into a room. It was very good timing on McKenzie's part of throwing up at the doctor's office, because we would have waited a lot longer than we did. The doctor immediately gave her a strep test and thank god it turned out negative. It turns out she has a viral flu and should be better in a few days. I thanked the lady who helped me out as I left. Even though McKenzie still doesn't feel well, I have the self-assurance she doesn't have strep. I brought her home and put her right to bed. That is how life is sometimes. Everything can be going along smoothly without any problems, then all of sudden it hits without warning and your life can change dramatically forever in a minute's time.

My family has lived through tragedy. Not my mother's current battle with cancer, but the death of my sister's second born child, Steven.

I am not exactly sure what Steven's heart problem was, but when he was born the doctors had told my sister that he would have to have surgery when he was two years old for him to grow and have a normal life. From the time he was born he was on medication and had to see several doctors. I was eighteen years old and just started my freshman year in college when Steven went into the hospital to have his surgery. I was already coming home that weekend because it was a holiday weekend so everything was working out that I would be able to be with my family after this ordeal. I called home to see how surgery went and my mom told me everything went fine. My trip home took anywhere from 5 to 6 hours, since my college was three hundred miles from home. So all the way home I didn't even think twice about Steven and just enjoyed the ride home. When I opened the door to my house my mother was there to greet me, she obviously looked like she was crying, she then hugged me. She told me little Steven passed away. I was shocked and devastated to put it mildly. What happened I thought to myself? I thought everything was fine? There were complications after surgery and while he was recovering his heart failed him. My sister and her husband were still at the hospital making arrangements as my parents and I sat there looking lifeless. My dad sent me out for coffee as I gladly went. I wanted to get out of the house. What am I going to say to my sister? What can I say? What is there to say when a mother loses a child at the precious age of two?

The next few days had to be some of the worst days of my life of thirty-one years. My sister held up pretty well. The wake was awful, there couldn't of been a dry eye in the house. When it was time to say our final good-byes, that is when it got really ugly. My sister broke down hard, and there was nothing that we could do to help her. It was good for her to let it all out, as she will never see her son again, until it is her time to reunite with him at another time and place.

Throughout the agonizing days of the wake and funeral, I never cried or showed any emotion. I felt horrible for my sister, and would do anything in the world to bring back Steven for her, but I could never feel the pain she felt losing a child, until now. What did I know about the love you share raising and bonding with your own flesh and blood. I was eighteen and in college drinking beers and chasing women. My life was just beginning. I could not and did not know what was going through my sister's mind as she had just had to bury a child of hers. I finally did break down on the way back to college. Since I stayed a few days past the holiday I had to take a train back because my ride left a few days earlier. I got ripped. I drank as much as my body could and sat on that train wondering and asking god many times over and over "why?" Why does god take small children like he took Steven? That ride back to school changed my whole outlook on life and God.

Looking back now some thirteen years later and with two children of my own, I can now sense what pain and suffering my sister must of gone through the day she had to bury Steven. I bet there isn't a day that goes by that she doesn't think about him. My whole existence in life would end if something tragic happens to one of my precious daughters. There is a saying the worst thing in life is having to bury your children, and it has to be true. I love and cherish them so much and if God decided to take one of them before I am already gone, I could not go on with life. I really believe that I could not be as strong as my sister was and I would totally lose it. I hear about children dying all the time and now that I am a father and I am with them every minute of the day, my heart goes out to anyone that must endure losing a child not only an early age, but at any age. With the way the world is today, having children is a risk. Crime and the way people just seem to be nowadays, it will be a gamble every time one of my daughters leave the house. I will pray and hope that God will be watching over them for their safe return. I now cry for my sister's loss as I couldn't cry for her then.

Week 23
March 8th-12th

Tuesday

Josie has turned into the "demon child" I expected. I knew that child raising couldn't be as easy as it was with McKenzie. Josie has arrived with a vengeance and is paying us back what we missed with McKenzie. Josie does all the things McKenzie never did that most children do when they are 10 months old and are able to crawl. She goes into all the cabinets and takes everything out. She loves to stick her head in the toilet. She grabs the toilet paper and pulls it out all over the floor. She pokes you in the eye, grabs your hair, and screams if she doesn't get her way and much more. She loves to go halfway up the stairs, turn back to see if Lisa or I are watching, then laughs and continues to go up the stairs faster for you to chase her. I began to pack some boxes for our move and she was able to peel off the moving tape off the boxes I sealed. That tape is on there like glue, but Josie was able somehow to peel it off, I couldn't believe it. She is trouble and is going to be trouble as she grows up. McKenzie will be the honor student and the prom queen, Josie will be on the wrestling team and know her principal on a first name basis. She is fearless, nothing really stops her. Within an hour she closed one of her fingers in a closet door and another finger got smashed on the lever of the gate I put up to stop her from falling down the stairs. She is a riot to watch and has a great personality. It is amazing how different personalities Josie and McKenzie have from each other. People of course blame me for the way Josie is. "It's your fault, you're home with her all day" and "she is just like you, trouble." Isn't that nice but I kind of like it. I comment to Lisa all the time that we have an angel and a devil. She doesn't like it when I call Josie the devil but I am only kidding. So I came up with another saying. McKenzie is the "good", Josie is the "bad" and Lisa is the "ugly." She doesn't like that either. I won't have anyone else to blame but myself if Josie turns out to be trouble, but it will be fun watching her grow up having fun the way I did. I got away with a lot with my parents and it will be interesting how much the girls get away with. It will be tough for them to do so, I believe I know every trick in the book.

Thursday

Summertime and this move to Atlanta cannot come soon enough. McKenzie has become very bored as of late being locked inside the house. I don't blame her. We have been cooped up in the house now going on five months and there is so much you can do before you get bored or tired of doing the same thing over and over. The computer games we have given her have worn off. She has pretty much mastered them and finds them no longer challenging, so her computer time is very limited. She doesn't even ask to watch any Barney tapes anymore. I thought I would never see the day that she didn't want to watch a Barney tape. Puzzles, books, coloring, these entire things do not interest her anymore. She needs to get outside and ride a bike or kick a ball. With our new house she will have her own swing set and slide in the backyard. There is a lot more room to run around inside and out. It will be better for all of us. Another key is Josie. Once Josie is able to walk and run around with McKenzie, those two should be able to keep each other occupied for hours at a time so Daddy can practice his golf swing. It is already happening. Josie and McKenzie roll around on the floor together and I see McKenzie trying to get Josie more involved in what she is doing. As it is turning out, having two girls this close in age couldn't have worked out better. They will be the best of friends and should occupy each other during the day so Daddy can do other things to have somewhat of a life. You wouldn't think that weather would be a factor when raising kids, but it does. You want good weather to be able to be outside and see other human beings and not feel like you are all alone on the planet raising two kids. Let me tell you, after a few days of spending all of your time inside the house with your kids, it can feel like you are all alone, and the only thing that keeps your sanity is nap time.

Week 24
March 15th-19th

Monday

McKenzie's new fad is umbrellas. I guess I better get used of my children going through fads and phases in life. I don't know how many times I am going to hear, "I must have it, everyone at school has it!" Another favorite will be "if I don't get to have it, I am going to die!" That is when I am going to have real fun with the girls. I am sure their styles in clothing is going to drive me nuts. Another nail in my coffin will be their hair. Wonder which one will come home first with blue hair? That will make my hair gray. So I will have to get even with them or at least let them suffer a little bit. As much as I am an antagonist, I will let them go through a little bit of hell and torture before I give into their wants. I say "wants" because whatever they will be begging and pleading for I am sure it will be nothing they will need just want because everyone else either has it or wants it. I will eventually give in and let them have whatever they have been belly aching about for days, because I am the greatest dad on the planet. Anyways, McKenzie has been wanting an umbrella now for a few weeks. Why? I don't know but I did buy her one this weekend. It is a red Teletubbie umbrella with her favorite Teletubbie, Poe, on the handle. She absolutely loves it and makes me hang it on her bedpost so she knows where it is at all times. She practices opening it up in the house (I know it is bad luck to open umbrellas inside, but how I am going to explain that to her) and walks around so proud. It is funny how a little thing like an umbrella can make someone so happy. With her being so happy, it makes me so happy. I enjoy so much giving to my kids, I would give them everything in the world if I could, even if it left me pennyless, but the smile on their faces would make me the richest man in the world. So now all we need is some rain for McKenzie to actually use her umbrella outside instead of pretending it is raining inside the house, but I can wait, I hate rain.

Wednesday

Teething has begun again for Josie. This will be her second time going through it. She didn't take well to her first round, but she seems to be holding up better this time around. Josie doesn't want anything to do with her bottle.

All the other signs are also there; slight fever, rosy cheeks, chewing on everything and of course, the green runniest stinkiest diapers that make me gag every time I open one up. On Monday alone, every time she woke up from one of her naps, as soon as I opened her door, the stench slapped me in the face as if I pinched a woman's butt in a strip bar. On Monday Josie soiled three onesie's, two outfits and a pair of pajamas. They are currently soaking in a bucket of soap trying to get the stench out. If the army can bottle up Josie's diapers, they would have a new chemical weapon hand. It is bad, real bad. It isn't even like a real bowel movement, I call it liquid gas. I read somewhere that teething is one of the most painful and hardest things a child has to go through. I guess they get even with us by making us change those disgusting diapers. Who would ever figure that getting teeth is such a big ordeal? It is amazing what changes and affects the body goes through when growing. I am glad that she is handling her teething a lot better this time than the first, but I am not. I have to brace myself before entering her room after she awakens. I know what is waiting for me and I am afraid, very afraid. I can say this because she is my daughter, she stinks!

Friday

"Twenty four weeks have come and past,
They have been precious moments I wish
I could cork in a bottle and make them last,

Twenty little fingers,
Twenty tiny toes,
Dirty diapers and pretty hair bows,

This is my life now
And wonderful it is,
As my two darling daughters
Have brought me nothing but bliss."

Week 25
March 22nd-26th

Tuesday

Misery and despair have once again struck the Major household; we are all sick together. McKenzie and Josie have ear infections, Mommy and Daddy have a slight touch of the flu. It all started Sunday night when Josie would not go to sleep for the night. All she did was cry. Lisa tried to put her down but she would just sit up in her crib and cry very hard. Of course Lisa and I believed it was her teeth. She has two right now and should be getting more any day, so we assumed she was teething. Lisa was finally able to get her to fall asleep around 10 pm It didn't last long, around 10:30 pm Josie woke up once again in a complete rage of tears. Lisa grabbed her and brought her into our bed. I can honestly say we never bring our kids into our bed. Our bed to me is our sanctuary, the forbidden territory for children. I am a strong believer that children should not sleep, or even play in the master bedroom. Of course there are always extreme circumstances that a child may need to sleep with their parents, and Lisa and I agreed that Josie needed to sleep with her mom for any of us to get any sleep at all. Josie slept on Lisa until 1:30am. After a couple of hours of Josie kicking me in the back it was time for her to go back in her crib. I gave her some Tylenol and she finally slept til the morning without waking up again. McKenzie has never slept in our bed. I believe it is just a bad habit to start and I will not allow it to. Monday morning arrived and McKenzie complained her ear hurt. Of course we all know what that means, ear infection. If she has one, sure enough Josie has one too. So without further delay, Lisa made a doctor's appointment for later in the day. Of course she was able to leave the "house of horror" and leave me with two sick children. She admitted she was happy to be going to work because being home with two sick kids, being sick yourself, is worse than having your eyebrows plucked out one hair at a time. I was able to muddle through the day as best I could, wiping nostril after nostril and holding Josie til my back broke. Lisa was able to come home early and take McKenzie to the doctor's office for the prescription of amoxicillin. Amoxicillin is pink gold for parents. If I was a pharmacist, I would sell gallons of amoxicillin on the black market. Now it is just sit back and wait for the amoxicillin to kick in and get us all on the road to recovery. Even though I am miserable, the kids are miserable, and my wife is miserable, I still wouldn't trade places with anyone. Wiping noses and shoving medicine down my kids throats is paradise, compared to having to go to work. When I am healthy and feeling good again, I must not think of work, because then I will get sick all over again.

Friday

Hell week is just about over as it is now Friday afternoon. Everyone in the house has been sick all week, with myself getting the brunt of it. I had it the worst (or am I just the biggest baby of them all). I don't know, I was the only one with a constant cough and never ending sneezes. The girls bounced back right away as soon as the amoxicillin kicked in. As for me and Lisa, we just suffered through it like the soldiers suffered through the cold winter during the American Revolution. Lisa had to perform at work all week (go poopie) which she very rarely ever does, but when you have diarrhea you have no choice but to go when nature calls. I would assume this is just the tip of the iceberg of things to come. I can see McKenzie and Josie getting the chicken pox together, flu's, colds and whatever else nature can throw at us. I can see them playing a lot together and being very close to each other as sisters. It is happening already as they play together on the floor. Before when Josie was just beginning to crawl, she was a nuisance to McKenzie. McKenzie would always push her and tell to go "go away." Now that Josie is a little bit older, McKenzie encourages Josie to play with her and they are much more interactive with each other. They play together with the doll house, they wrestle, chase each other and so on. So when one of them gets sick, it won't take long for the other to pass the germs right over. In a sense I won't mind. I would rather them both be sick together, than one be sick one week, and the other the next, especially with the chicken pox. Let both get it together and get the misery over with in one shot. McKenzie and Josie will not only be sisters, they will be best friends. I'm not going to lie about it, but when Lisa got pregnant the second time, I was hoping it was a boy. Not because I am a man and I have a macho thing going that I must have a son, but this way we would have one boy and one girl and call it a night. Instead we have two girls 23 months apart, and what seems to be a growing bond between McKenzie and Josie, Lisa and I couldn't be happier. I am very content with my two daughters and I try to convince Lisa of it all the time. She would still like three, but that will not be. Maybe?

Monday

The girls are healthy again, Lisa thinks she is pregnant, I think I might have bronchitis and we are 12 days away from moving. It is very chaotic and stressful right now at the Major house. My wife thinks she is pregnant because over the weekend she has been nauseous and even threw up. First of all, I told her we would have had to have sex to get pregnant (sex is pretty much non-existence right now, I'll get into that subject later) and she is just sick from nerves and stress. Experts say moving is one of the most stressful things a family can go through and I have to agree. With me being sick just adds fuel to the fire. It is my own fault; I won't see a doctor. I don't know why? Lisa yells at me everyday to see a doctor, but my ego won't allow it. Am I really that stupid? My wick is very short and my blood pressure has to be off the chart. I am snapping at every little thing that goes wrong, and yelling at the girls for no real good reason. It is taking all the patience I have to get through this move and I really don't have a lot left at this moment. Our house is full of boxes and is a complete mess all the time. Lisa has three days of work left but I wish she took off more time to help me out. She has done everything she can at night, but when she comes home she has the girls until they go to bed, then she is really too tired to do much. I don't blame her and that is why I am trying to get everything done during the day. My antibodies have really taken a beating, I should have been over my sickness a week ago. McKenzie is very bored as she watches a lot of TV, but when we move the TV watching will decrease enormously as we will be too busy running around settling into our new house. Plus, our new house is so much bigger; the girls will have plenty of space to mess around. I already know that the double entry staircase leading upstairs will act like a playground. That is why I spent the extra money to upgrade the carpet to make is kid proof. We will see how long it lasts before McKenzie and Josie wear it out to the floor. We also decided to throw McKenzie a third birthday party before we leave. We thought this would be a good idea because when her birthday comes in May, she really won't have any friends yet we would be able to invite to a party, so we decided to have it early so she can have all her friends from the neighborhood come. We also planned Josie's first birthday party this weekend. We are just inviting our immediate families and we are having it at a restaurant. Our heads are spinning like tops and sometimes we don't know which direction to go to first. We have so much to do and so little time. We both agree once the dust settles and life gets back to normal, life should be pretty good to us. Unless Lisa is pregnant then life is just mean. She probably hopes she is pregnant so she doesn't have to help move any of the boxes, it would be just like her to pull something like that.

Wednesday

I couldn't take it anymore; I finally went to see a doctor regarding my illness. About halfway through yesterday I was no longer able to bend over or even tilt my head in the down direction. It felt like my head was being squeezed in a vice and King Kong was turning the handle. It took every ounce of will in my body to make it through the day. It turns out I have a severe sinus infection. I have never had one before and hope to god I never get one again. I don't get sick much, but I knew something serious had to be wrong with me for me to be sick for almost two weeks and getting worse by the day. The last time I felt this horrible was back in college when I came down with mononucleosis. I wasn't 100 percent for a month. I don't have a month to wait; I need to get better now!

Not only did I go to the doctor for myself; I also went for the sake of my family. I have not been very pleasant to be around. I am surprised that Lisa hasn't filed for divorce and fled with the girls. I hope my girls still love me. I have been no fun and my tolerance level has been below zero. Everyday for lunch I give McKenzie a juice box. Today she was playing with the straw and accidently dropped the box off the table and landed on Josie that was playing nearby. Josie wasn't fazed at all but did get a little juice on her clothes. I totally went out of control yelling and screaming towards McKenzie. The whole tirade lasted about 10 minutes all for an accidental drop of a little juice box. I treated McKenzie as if she committed murder. I felt horrible afterwards as my heart broke as I stared at her glossy tear-filled eyes. Right there and then I called to make an appointment to see the doctor. I begged for McKenzie's forgiveness as I tried to explain to her that "Daddy" is not felling well and it wasn't her fault that I yelled at her the way I did. I gave myself a timeout and basically kissed her butt like there was no tomorrow until she took her nap. I also find myself yelling at Josie. She is only 11 months old, am I an idiot? Whenever I finish yelling at McKenzie , I always feel like I just killed my best friend. It breaks my heart to see the disappointing look on her face. Is she disappointed in me or herself? I don't know? I remember when my dad used to get into moods like the one I am in now and it was no fun being around him. My dad could be very intimidating when he wanted to be. I don't want my girls to ever be afraid of me. I don't want to be one of those dads that just scream and yell and discipline their children. I want my girls to know that their father is more that just a parent, I also want them to know I am their friend. I will never wait this long again to see a doctor once I become sick. I cannot be the father I want to be when I can't even be the human being I want to be. I know this doesn't mean much now to McKenzie and Josie, but Daddy is very sorry.

Friday

Today is Good Friday for Catholics, but to me it is "Great Friday." Lisa's last day of work was yesterday so she will be home with us until April 12th when she starts her new job with her new company in Atlanta. Little does she know that I am officially "off duty" the next twelve days as I try to get this house packed up and ready to move. The time she has missed with her girls will be made up real fast; as she will get the brunt of taking care of the them. It couldn't come at a better time. I need a break from them and I need to concentrate on something else. My sinus infection is still lingering around as I am not yet 100 percent. I don't want to touch a bottle, or change a diaper or watch anymore Barney for next 12 days. I am on vacation in my own mind and in my own world. See you on the beach.

Week 27
April 5th- 9th
(Moving week)

Monday

At the end of this week a new beginning will begin. This week will consist of boxes, newspaper, packing tape, goodbyes, tears and everlasting memories. I am predicting a difficult week, due to the many tasks and minute details that are involved in moving, then throw in the mix that I still have to care for two small children. Lisa will pretty much handle the girls, as I will box everything I can throughout the house. I keep asking McKenzie what box she wants to go in. She believes she and Josie are going to be packed away in a box and put on the truck. She is ok with it, she tells me she will feed Josie, but will not change her diaper because "she stinks." She also reminds me that I must poke holes in the box so she can get some air. She is not afraid, I would be. Everyday more and more memories within the house will begin to disappear into boxes.

Tuesday

McKenzie has been on my butt to make sure all her stuff is coming to the new house. All I hear all day is "Is my bed coming to the new house?" of course it is I answer. "Are my toys coming to the new house?" of course they are I answer again, and again, and again. This conversation goes on all day. I have to make this transition as smooth as possible since McKenzie seems to be unhappy about us moving. She has good reasons to be upset as we are moving away from the only house she has known. It has to be scary, I never moved when I was growing up. The only time I moved was when I was 21 years old and I moved in with Lisa, then my fiancee. A lot of thoughts must be going through her mind, as many are going though mine. I am sure McKenzie and I share the same thoughts. Are we going to meet new friends? Are we going to like our new house? Will we miss our families and friends? I am 31 years old and she is only going to be 3 and we have the same worries. I find that amazing. It has to be confusing for her as to "why" we are moving when she is very happy right where she is. We are happy too, but we want to be as happy as we can possibly be, and that is why we are moving. She does acknowledge that she is moving away from her friends and family, but we assured her she will make new friends and see her family as much, if not more than we do now. She has mentioned many times she doesn't want to move to the new house, in which put a lump in my throat. The last thing I want to do is upset McKenzie during this transition. We are very confident once the dust clears and we are settled in our new house and McKenzie has new friends, she will forget all about this time of in-between and be the happy little girl that I know and love.

Friday

People came by all week to say their goodbyes and to wish us luck. Everyone has said they will miss us, but also stated we are doing the right thing. That has reassured Lisa and I that we are making the right decision. We haven't thought much about how this is going to affect our lives so much, but we have been worried about the girls. Josie is too young to even have a clue what is happening, and within time McKenzie should be perfectly fine. After our closing we packed our van with everything we would need for the next six days. Our van is packed from the top to bottom, from front to rear. There was barely enough room to fit in the two girls and Brodie. Of course if it were up to Lisa, Brodie would have been left behind. I have to keep reminding her that Brodie is her first born like it or not. We look like the Clampetts moving to Beverly Hills. We have our plants, luggage, dog food, blankets, toys, tools, portable crib, and countless baby formula packed in the van. We even have a mirror and glass shelves we didn't trust putting in the moving van. To top it off I have my wave runner and trailer hitched on to the back. We will spend a couple of days with our families before making our journey down to Atlanta. When it is time to go, I know my wife will cry, but I hope I won't, unless someone steals our van, then I will most definitely cry.

Sunday

   Houston, we have touched down. The major shuttle has landed safely in
Atlanta, not without a couple of scary moments. We left on time, 9 pm on
Saturday. Before we left we had our last dinner with my mom and dad for
who knows how long. My mom looks ok, but she is not the same. She has no
appetite and barely eats anything. She had maybe five spoon-fulls of her soup
and had about five bites of her chicken stir-fry. It makes me sick to see my
mother deteriorate the way she is. She is the most unselfish person I have
ever known. She could be all over me not to move away because of her
condition, but she insists that I go and be happy. I remember growing up; she
gave us kids everything and she never put herself first before any on us. After
all these years she is still the same way. This could have been one of the last
meals I ever sit down my mother before she gets too sick. If I didn't move
because of her, she would be very upset and that is the last thing I want to do
right now. I love her very much and I hope she knows that. My father was
totally against us leaving at night, but I didn't want to travel 700 hundred
miles with a 3 year, a 1 year old and a dog in the middle of the day. Lisa and
I both agreed the best thing for us to do is travel at night so the girls would
sleep right through the misery of the long drive. I was on the first shift and
drove with no problem for the first four hours. We stopped for gas and Lisa
took over. Just like every time the girls sleep in the van, as soon as it stops
they wake up. They did but I knew they would go right back to sleep. We
gassed up as Lisa got back on the highway when all of a sudden that smell
that I cannot tolerate hit me like a slap in the face; McKenzie threw up all
over herself and her car seat. Thank God there was an exit about two miles
down the road as we had to make an emergency stop to clean her and the seat
up of throw up. Of course I had that duty as Lisa took McKenzie inside the
gas station to change her. Josie just sat in her car seat just smiling and
laughing at me. She thought it was just hilarious that I am stuck in the middle
of nowhere at 1am cleaning up throw up, I however begged to differ. That
little mishap took about twenty minutes and we were back on the road. Lisa
then drove the next 3 hours as I took a nap. As I took my second shift, every
mile I counted my blessings that nothing terrible has gone wrong. I couldn't
think of anything worse than being stranded at the side of the rode, in the

middle of t he night with two small children out in the middle of nowhere. Then the unthinkable happened, about 400 miles into our journey the check engine light goes on. My heart dropped into my stomach as all I can do is stare at it and say, "Please God, let us make it safely." I couldn't help stare at it as it glowed in the night like a burning meteorite heading towards earth. My palms began to sweat as thoughts of doom race through my mind. Then I began to rationalize. The engine is probably just running hot since it has never been on this long of a trip. Was I really rationalizing or trying to convince myself everything was going to be all right? I looked over next to me as I see my wife sleeping hoping she doesn't awake, I don't want her to panic. All I can do is keep driving and pray nothing does happen.

We make it to morning and daylight has arrived. We stop for breakfast about two hours away as I hope the van cools down and the check engine light will shut itself off. We are in the restaurant for about an hour as I took my time. The whole time I was in there I was hoping two things; one, the van would start and two the engine would be cooled so I don't have to stare at the check engine light for another 150 miles. No luck, still glowing like the Olympic torch. All I can do is continue to drive and hope for the best. The best was good enough as we pulled into my friend's driveway to drop off the wave runner. I thanked God as I kissed the ground for a safe trip as I also gave my two daughters kisses and thanked god for our safe trip. The next couple of days we will be spending in a hotel room. That shouldn't be too bad, two adults, two children, one dog, a van loaded with stuff in a room the size of a bedroom. God gives hope, God takes it away.

Monday

There is an old joke or expression that goes something like "my room is so small, I need to leave it to change my mind." Well that is how tight we are all in this hotel room. The room consists of a queen size bed, a TV, a small kitchen and a bathroom. All of this is fitting in a room about the size of a bedroom. Include two adults, two children, a dog and a van full of stuff, I feel like the jelly oozing out of a donut. This situation couldn't be worse. After driving 700 hundred miles we are now condemned to this cell for almost three days. This is really going to test the patience of Lisa and I, mostly me since Lisa is actually the lucky one that is able to escape Alcatraz by going to work. I can't believe I am going to say this but I actually envy her for going to work. I will not be able to spend all day in this room with the girls and the dog. I have to drive Lisa to work at 8 am since our other vehicle will not be here until we close on the new house in three days. When I drop her off, the girls and I will spend the day driving, shopping, and going to our new house and whatever else it takes to get us through the day. I have about 6 hours to kill before the girls need a nap. I figure if I can stall until 2 pm and put the girls down along with myself, 5 pm should come quickly as Lisa will be out of work to relieve me. This will test the patience for both of us as Brodie is already barking at every car door she hears, and the girls have nothing else to do but play with the buttons on the air conditioner. I have stopped them a couple of times already, but to be honest, they have nothing else to do so I am just going to let them play with it. I know they will both come down with head colds or something from the cold air, but I really don't have any other choice. We are all prisoners waiting to get paroled and whatever passes the time by, I encourage it.

Tuesday

One more day, I can make it one more day. The walls are closing in around me and I question my existence in life. Is this what claustrophobics feel like? I watch the clock with excitement as every minute ticks by. I can make it, I know I can. Can I? I must! I will never take my house for granted because as bad as I have it right now, there are families out there that have it worse off. I reflect on how grateful and lucky we are that we are able to move into a new house. We have worked hard and sacrificed a lot, but I do count my blessings everyday for a healthy family and pretty good fortune. One more day, one more day!

Wednesday

Our prison term is over and we are all free to go. We are all pretty excited but McKenzie keeps saying she wants to go home. In time that will pass, but right now it is not easy to swallow when she says that. The last couple of days have been rough but now they will only get better. McKenzie is just about 3 years old but she is very sensitive and is very aware of what is happening. She knows she is far away from home and will no longer see her friends she has made the short time she has been on earth. In time she will make new friends and have a very good life herself. I hope we all do because if I have to spend anymore time in a hotel room like we did the last few days, I will be carried away by men in little white coats as I rubbed my finger up and down between my lips.

Friday

Life is good again. We have a lot of work ahead of us, but we are in our new house and we have nothing else to look forward to but the future. McKenzie was very excited running through the house picking out the room she wanted. If she only knew we already designated which room she got and luckily she picked out the room we wanted her to have, she is amazing. When I was putting Josie's crib back together she was jumping and smiling like an ape staring at a bunch of bananas. She hasn't slept in her crib for a week now and she can't wait to get back in it. As I unpacked McKenzie's dolls, toys and stuffed animals she was very thrilled to have them back and in her bed. Life will slowly get back to normal for all of us and it cannot come soon enough. Everyday the girls will get adjusted to the new surroundings along with Lisa and I. McKenzie has mentioned a few more times she wants to go back to the old house but I figure it is for attention and that should pass in time. We will all be able to live much more comfortably in this house compared to the old house. The old house was very good to us, a lot of memories will always stay with Lisa and I as the two most important moments happened there; the bringing home of our two precious daughters. There will be thousands of memories that will come from this house, some good, some bad, but the only thing Lisa and I will bring home to this house today will be a pizza.

Week 29
April 19th-23rd

Monday

Life is back to normal if there is such a thing. Lisa went to work and I got back into the routine of going to the grocery store. I was a little nervous going the first time. At our old grocery store McKenzie would always get a cookie from the baker, and knowing McKenzie's elephant like memory, she will be looking for a cookie with no one there to give her one. As we walked through the automatic doors, I spotted something better than a cookie; the store has toy shopping carts for the kids to push around and act like real shoppers. McKenzie grabbed one and started pushing it just like like Daddy. She loved it as I started to put food inside her cart like mine. No requests for a cookie, she was too involved in her shopping cart as she looked adorable going down the aisles shopping like her Daddy. It brought a huge smile to my face and hers, as I know shopping will once again be enjoyable. It will be things like this that will make McKenzie stop asking to go back to the old house. When we left the store to go home McKenzie asked me when would we go shopping again. I asked her if she liked her shopping cart and she replied with an enthusiastic "yes!" If I could only give the store a high five because the toy shopping cart saved the day.

Wednesday

Life for me is chaos right now. I have a new house, with a garage full of boxes that I have to unpack, I have workers from the builder fixing problems with the house, and all of this wrapped around the care of my two daughters. I wish there was someone here I knew that could watch the girls for a few hours so I can rip through the boxes and try to get this house in order. McKenzie really isn't the problem, it's Josie. She is a little terror. She is nothing like McKenzie was at her age; Josie gets herself into everything. I can't take my eyes off her for two seconds without her going up the stairs or getting into something. I thought one of the advantages with having a bigger house would be the girls would have more space to run around and play. Well they do, but that also brings more responsibility on my part to pay more attention and watch them more carefully. It takes me longer to get to them now than before since the house is bigger, and there is more house for them to get in trouble than before. So far Josie has crawled inside the fireplace, crawled up the stairs about 50 times (in which I cannot block off since my security gate is in the other truck), climbed up a ladder to the attic, gone inside the kitchen cabinets and pulled out the pots and pans. All of this in just three days. What amazes me she can do all of these things but yet will not walk. McKenzie walked at nine months. At the rate Josie is going she will be nine years old before she walks. She gets around good enough on her hands and knees to accommodate herself so she isn't really interested in walking. She walks fine with her walker and on the furniture but on her own, forget it. She will just let go and plop down on her butt and take off like a turtle out of water. Actually, she can take her time walking because once she is able to walk, she will be even more trouble than she already is now. She will set McKenzie on fire or electrify herself as soon as she gets herself more mobile. It's funny when they fight, McKenzie right now is getting the better of it, but Josie tries to fend her off by biting her with her two teeth. I know it is a bad habit to start, but Josie knows that is her only way of defending herself and it cracks me up when McKenzie yells that Josie is biting her. McKenzie is in big trouble when Josie grows up and she will be able to really defend herself against her big sister. I'll bring the girls to the park later today and tomorrow to help McKenzie adjust. She loved going to the park at the old house so this should be a way of bribing her. I haven't heard today that she wanted to go back to the old house so I am feeling a lot better she has not mentioned it. I have to go, Josie is now playing in Brodie's water dish. Josie, stop it! No!

Friday

Battle of the sexes: I am getting a little tired of people coming up to me and stating "you have to go for the boy". Meaning you want me to conceive another child, have my wife carry a baby for nine months, go through labor and delivery and still have a 50-50 percent chance of having a boy, just so I can have a boy. Why do people insist you must have children of both sexes? If I do have another child and it is a girl, what then, we must go for four? No way! I am very content and happy with my two lovely daughters. What if I had two sons instead? Would I be content? Probably. I am not going to have a litter of children just to have children of both sexes. Having same sex children doesn't mean you're going to miss something in life. Today I had to go to my friend's house to pick up my wave runner. When I got to his house no one would be home, but he left the garage door open for me to get into the garage where my wave runner was. McKenzie drank a full cup of juice on the way over, and nature is calling for her. I knocked on a couple of his neighbors doors, but to no avail. So I had to proceed with plan B, she would have to pee outside. This is usually stereotyped as a "male" activity, peeing outside. Well I just want to let everyone know that my daughter made Daddy very proud. I pulled her pants down, told her to squat like our dog Brodie and pee on the grass. She peed as easily outside as she does when she is on the potty. She really enjoyed it and couldn't wait to go home and tell Mommy she peed outside like Brodie. You see, girls can do whatever boys do as long as you teach them or get them involved. My brother, who is four years older than me, wasn't interested in sports at all when he was growing up. He probably couldn't even name a professional sports team in all of sports. Myself on the other hand was very involved in sports and watched all the sports teams on TV. Everyone is different and has different interests. It doesn't automatically mean if you're a boy you will be in sports and work on car engines (to this day I couldn't even change oil in a car if I had to) or ride a motorcycle. You will be involved in things that interest you as a person and also how much participation and interest your parents show with you. Some parents go overboard and push their children so hard into something, the child usually revolts against them. Parents should just sit back and find out what there children become interested in and then encourage them and become involved at a moderate level so everyone is comfortable. If parents don't show any interest in their children's activities, odds are the child will lose interest and give up or quit. That is neither good for the child or the parent. McKenzie and Josie will be encouraged to do whatever they want when they decide or become interested in something. If it is baseball, soccer, dance, music, etc., Lisa and I will let them know we are behind them 100 percent as long as they are. If McKenzie wants to become a plumber, she can, even though she is a girl. I will never discourage my girls from doing anything they want to do. They will try things they like, and don't like, that is for them to decide. I want them to try everything that interests them. It is better to try and fail, then to have never tried at all. In this day and age, there are no boundaries for sexes; unless it is the bathroom. Boys and girls are sharing a lot of the same interests compared to twenty years ago. I will not miss anything because I have two girls, in fact I will enjoy double to pleasure of have two wonderful daughters. It doesn't matter if you have a boy or a girl, or three of the same, the world of opportunity is open to whoever wants to walk in.

Saturday April 24th, 1999

At 8:30 pm tonight, Josie Samantha Major, will officially be one year old. I cannot believe my little "snookers" is a year old already. I can go on and on what Josie means to me, and what she has brought into my life, but that would just get redundant. I just want to wish my little girl the happiest birthday a father can wish. Happy Birthday Josie, Daddy loves you very much.

"A year ago today, I got a gift from god above,
A blue eyed, blue face, pudgy being only a father could love,
A year has past,
Why does the time fly past?
Even thought the time doesn't last,
The memories you will give to me throughout your lifetime
Will always be cherished in my heart of mine."

Tuesday

The bribery is beginning to work. Last night we went to a home improvement store and bought McKenzie her play set for the backyard. She is very exited and anxious. The wood for it was delivered and is sitting in our driveway. McKenzie just stares out the window looking at it asking Daddy "when can I play on it?" That is a good question since the play set is just a bunch of wooden boards of nut and bolts. Daddy took care of everything though. While we were picking out the play set we liked, I inquired about the assembly fee. To much of my surprise it was 80 percent of the cost of the equipment itself. I don't have any tools or time let alone the patience to put this play set together. It is so very important that we get this play set up as fast as possible for McKenzie, plus I wanted to make sure it wouldn't fall apart after she was done playing with it. I thought very seriously just paying the amount of getting it assembled. I figured I would just go down to the mission to donate blood for the next 10 years. God was looking down on me again as I began talking to the salesman on how ridiculous the price of the construction was. I began acting sad and disappointed that McKenzie wouldn't have her play set anytime soon. He then mentioned to me he has put a few of these together in the past and would do it himself for a fraction of the cost. I began to get very excited as we worked out the details as I wanted to kiss him on the lips. We worked out a "very good" price between us and within a matter of days McKenzie should have an erect, well-built play set in her very own backyard. Since the purchase of the play set, even though it is just a pile of wood and bolts, no comments from her wanting to go back to the old house. The play set we have promised her is almost a reality. So I have learned two lessons: bribery can make children happy and forgetful, and giving people the sad puppy eye look work in your advantage especially when kids are involved. He thought he was the salesman, I believe I was the salesman getting him to build our play set for a fraction of the cost. Chalk another one up for "Super Dad."

Friday

Lisa was a couple of days late in getting her period this month. She was worried, I on the other hand could only laugh. I don't know how many times I need to say it, but "you have to have sex in order to become pregnant." The last 6 weeks, I could count on one hand (excluding the thumb) how many times Lisa and I have made love. I would usually put the blame totally on her, but I am part of the blame as well. With all the packing, the move, the girls and all the stress that has come with this experience, we have both been exhausted by the time we would have anytime alone to be with each other. That stops right here, right now! We are all settled in, her new job is going well and the girls are back on schedule. It is time to get busy breaking in our new house, room by room, day by day, whatever it takes to reacquaint ourselves with each other. It will be tough and it will be a challenge, but it is a challenge I welcome with open arms. I am currently reading a book on sex and there is a quote in the book stating "two young kids is the best birth control method possible." I have to agree to a point, but I can honestly say that my sex drive is still in fifth gear. Lisa's sex drive is either in neutral or reverse most of the time. There are two main reasons for her motor being stuck. One is she spends all day at work, then comes home and spends all night with the girls. The girls go to bed relatively late since Lisa wants to spend as much time with them as she can being she is at work all day and doesn't get the chance most mothers do. The later the girls go to bed, the more tired Lisa becomes. Second, Lisa is totally off limits while the girls are awake. I try to grab her and fondle her when the kids are not looking, but Lisa will have nothing to do with it. She always yells "not when the kids are awake." I keep asking her if we could just slip away inside a closet for two minutes? I figure since she is too tired almost every night to do the horizontal bop, I should get her when she is awake, right? Wrong, I strike out every time. My hope right now is the house. We broke in every room in our old house, even the garage and the attic, so I am hoping the same with our new house. If that is going to be the case, Lisa and I should be a couple of pretty busy rabbits in the next few weeks. I am very excited, unless of course, Lisa states next month she is late again with her period, and with all the sex I think I am going to have, then we will never have sex again. Not because of Lisa, but what I will do to myself with the weed wacker in the garage. Ouch!

Week 31
May 3rd- 7th

Monday

I have come to the conclusion that all subdivisions are nothing more than big gossip mills. This past Saturday our subdivision hosted a spring barbecue. Lisa and I were excited about going since we just moved here and this would be a good step in meeting new people. We also hoped that McKenzie could make some new friends as well. As we arrived at the barbeque we were all a little nervous. We arrived a little late and there had to been 100 people already there staring us down coming up with their own conclusions about us in their heads. As Lisa and I began to drink, mingling with strangers became easier. McKenzie was having fun running around with the other kids her own age for the first time since we moved. That put a smile on my face watching her having fun again. I had Josie and Lisa was with McKenzie as we began to talk with our fellow neighbors. The conversations were mostly all the same: "We are you from?" "What do you do?" "Where do you live?" "How many children do you have?" Etc., etc. Everything was normal until a woman stopped Lisa out of nowhere and grabbed her hand and was very excited to meet Lisa. Granted she never met this person before, but she knew Lisa only because she was the only other woman in the subdivision, besides herself, that worked. How did she know this? Lisa told me she talked to maybe two or three people about our family situation and news sure did travel fast. The woman was very nice, but I am wondering what all the men are thinking about me. The women in the neighborhood know I stay home because I have been invited to a playgroup. I also found out that on Mondays you are able to drop off your children from 9:30am-12:30pm and have three hours to do whatever you want children free. I only have one word to describe that, golf! So within a couple of hours, the whole neighborhood knows that Lisa works, I stay home, we are from Chicago and have two girls. News spread faster in a subdivision than on the internet. I like our neighborhood though, they seem to have a lot of social functions to keep everyone involved and neighborly, or is it just a way for people to keep tabs on everyone. The Monday "drop off" is a gift from heaven. Where else can I drop off two children for three hours for free to do whatever I wanted? My only fee is that I will have to take my turn watching the children from the subdivision on a rotation basis. Life should be good here as long as I keep quiet and don't tell the neighbors any secret recipes. I have learned if you want news to travel fast, use a telephone or a telegraph, or better yet, tell a neighbor.

Thursday

The last couple of days have been designated "hold Josie days." It all started Monday night when Josie began running a fever. I thought to myself that Josie and I would be making our first visit to our new doctor real soon. In the middle of the night Josie woke up screaming. Lisa jumped out of bed as I just laid there thinking to myself how I hate the first visits to any kind of doctor offices. There are so many forms to fill out, in which people can't read anyways since my handwriting is so bad, plus I would be doing all this paperwork while holding Josie in one arm and corralling McKenzie with the other. I was not looking forward to that at all. So I laid there waiting for Lisa to get back in bed with any conclusions what might be wrong with Josie. Of course Lisa had no clue and we both just agreed that if the fever wasn't gone by tomorrow I would take her in to see the doctor. Josie woke up Tuesday still with a fever but with something else too, two brand new teeth. It never occurred to us that she was teething, she didn't have any of the other signs. Her diapers weren't seaweed green with a toxic smell and her cheeks weren't rosy. Anyways, there they were, two front teeth popping out of her gums like a turtle coming out its shell. She still was running a fever and just wanted to be held but at least now we know what was wrong with her. No doctors office visit yet, yes! Even though I didn't have to go to the doctor's office, the next couple of days were rough as Josie battled through the pain of getting two new teeth. Lisa told me she heard that if an adult had to go through the pain of getting new teeth, the pain is so severe that a person would have to be heavily sedated at all times. Poor Josie, such a good baby and she doesn't have a clue why she is in so much pain. I wish I could take the pain away from her and endure her pain myself, rather than see her battle through this torture. Last night she was so tired from crying that I was able to lay with her on the couch, as she cuddled up under my armpit and sucked her fingers till she fell asleep. One of the things I enjoy most about my girls is sleeping with them. I only sleep with them on certain occasions and I really love it. She just laid there so calmly as I stroked her hair and told her everything will be all right. Lisa confessed to me she was jealous that I was able to comfort her the way I did. I told Lisa Josie just preferred me over her since the past couple of I was home to hold her and comfort her through her ordeal. I always let Lisa put the girls to bed at night, but last night I wanted to put Josie down as she is finally over her teething.

It is times like this that I do think about having another child. Josie isn't a baby anymore and I will miss nights like this. Even though Josie cried most of the time, I knew that I and only I could calm her down and make everything all right. Josie will soon be walking and talking and going to college. If we decide not to have another child, Josie is it. I just embarked on a memory that will never be repeated. My babies are growing up faster than weeds in a garden. Stroking her hair and singing her to sleep makes me want to have more children, almost that is. At least I thought about.

Friday

Business as usual. Josie is back to being herself as her teeth have finally popped through thus making it normal once again at the home front. With this week being so laid back, the energy level within my body and the girls were on high as we needed to burn off some stored up energy. No better way than destroying the house together. It was really fun as we played hard and took no prisoners. It all started after lunch as McKenzie and I wrestled on the floor as Josie crawled on top of us trying to get into the action. Then Josie climbed onto her walker as McKenzie followed her around, and around, and around the staircase what seemed like hours. Then I started to chase them both around the staircase and would end up diving headfirst into Josie's new ball pit that we bought her for her birthday. It was fun as we would hit the pit and 200 balls would come crashing down all around us. Then I put the girls inside the pit and twisted and turned it like a hurricane. We played hard then we began to throw the balls at each other and whatever else we can find. The house was full of laughter and joy after a week of pain and sorrow. Let me digress for a moment; I could be having the time of my life with my daughters or I can be stuck in traffic commuting to work of trapped inside a cube trying to figure out why the company's balance sheet doesn't balance. Duh? I feel sorry for my wife having to work but somebody's got to do it and it's not going to be me. After we destroyed the house from playing, I laid the girls down for a rest as I took my position on the couch. I looked around at the mess and thought about cleaning it up, thought about it. I'll leave it here for Lisa to clean up so she can experience what I have to go through day after day. I don't know how I can take it anymore cleaning up after these kids? If she only knew. It was a good ending to the week from a bad beginning.

Week 32
May 10th-14th

Tuesday

My title of "full time dad" really took meaning the last two days because Lisa has been away on her first business trip with her new company. She was only gone for two days, but this was the first time in that I really had to take care of my girls all by myself for two full days. I thought that I would be dreading it, but to my surprise it was easier than expected. It is kind of hard to explain, but I felt much more at ease and calm taking care of the girls all by myself day and night, than when Lisa is there in the morning then comes home at night. I believe I felt this way because I had no other choice, I knew that it was I and only I to take care of the girls. It's like a back-up quarterback in football. During the game, the back-up quarterback is on the sidelines pacing nervously that at any minute he might be summoned into the game if the starting quarterback gets injured. He has no intentions on going into the game, but needs to be prepared if called to duty. If the back-up quarterback knew before the game that he was going to play instead of the starter, he would be much more prepared and ready to play than before just standing there watching. I knew I had no choice and no relief for the next couple of days. During a normal day, I watch the clock knowing anytime around 5:30 pm Lisa would be home to relieve me of duty. So I would watch the clock in anticipation and every minute past 5:30 pm, I start to get impatient thinking to myself "where is she, I wish she would hurry up and get home." Knowing Lisa wouldn't be home last night, I didn't watch the clock and I was very calm. The day went on as normal and the girls didn't miss a beat. McKenzie did ask when would Mom be home and I finally had to tell her she wouldn't be home until tomorrow at dinner time. We did not tell her on purpose knowing she would get upset and make the day harder on herself and me. Once I told her about her mom, her eyes got very teary and questioned me, "Why she wasn't coming home?" I explained it to her as softly as I could and she bounced right back. After dinner we went shopping for a couple of hours to get out of the house and to waste time before it was the girls bedtimes. Josie has been perfect (but I wouldn't expect anything less with me in charge) which has helped me tremendously. If Lisa had to go out of town when Josie was teething, the last couple of days could have been like Custards Last Stand. The girls went to bed on time and I had to whole house to myself. I stretched out on the couch, grabbed a bag of Fritos and watched my beloved Chicago Cubs lose. A rude ending to an otherwise perfectly good day.

Thursday

Some questions that I would like answered.

Why is it you give a child chocolate pudding for a snack and instead of eating it they use it as finger paint?

Why does a baby only take one sock off and leave the other one on?

Why is sharing in a child's mind a four letter word?

How does a baby make an odor so repulsive it can make a grown man cry?

How much are my daughters' weddings going to cost me?

Why is it every time your child needs to go to the bathroom right when your food comes at a restaurant?

Why are children so expensive? They are smaller than adults.

Can adults order from the children's menu? They always have better selections on theirs.

Why do babies crawl up the stairs 50 times a day before they realize they cannot get down?

Wouldn't it be great if women could give birth to babies that are six months old?

Can stay home parents collect unemployment when their kids go to school or move out of the house?

Why is it whenever you stand with your child in your arms, you have the uncontrollable urge to sway side to side?

Do children ask questions to learn or just to be annoying?

Why am I one of the luckiest men on the planet?

Week 33
May 17th-21st

Monday

If there ever was going to be a time were I would question my manhood or worry about what other people think of me staying home with my children as my wife works, today was going to be that day. About 2 weeks ago we received a flyer in our mailbox regarding a playgroup a mother down our street wants to start up. Lisa and I agreed that it would be great for the girls and a good way for Lisa and I to meet our new neighbors within the community. I was the one having to do the dirty work and go and meet all the mothers by myself without the help of my wife. Being the good father I am, I sucked it up and went for the goodness of my daughters to gain new friends. I was the second to arrive as I immediately felt out of place and uncomfortable. I knew going in I would be the only man there and I should be used to my role by now, but I couldn't help the feeling that was coming over me. It was easy when I was back at our old house and I knew everyone and everyone knew me, but here I am starting fresh and would have to explain to everyone why I am staying home, not my wife. There would be eleven mothers in total and countless children. McKenzie immediately began playing as Josie and I sort of slid into a corner by ourselves. I just laid back and listened for awhile as I prayed that no one would start talking about their menstrual cycle. I don't drink hard liquor very often, but if there were a bottle of booze in the room, I would have done a shot or two to loosen up. After about a half-hour some of the mothers began to introduce themselves to me. I am sure they had some reservations talking to me as I had talking to them. McKenzie and Josie were enjoying themselves so it was my turn to begin. I broke away from the corner and explained everything to everyone at least 5 times. All the mothers were very nice to me which was encouraging. Almost everyone there has moved here from somewhere else and is meeting each other for the first time. There was some gossip flying around the room as my ear stuck out a little further from my head to listen. I love gossip. I won't spread gossip, but I sure will soak it in. There was coffee and cupcakes as I sat back drinking and eating getting to know everyone in the group. We set up a schedule to meet every week with each one of us taking turns hosting that week's playgroup. Lisa will have to stay home that morning from work when it is my turn to host playgroup. I do cook, but I don't bake. Lisa will

96

have the duty of baking the goods. By the end of the two hours I felt much more comfortable and relaxed as the ice has been broken. McKenzie made some new friends and so did I. As time goes by I won't need to explain to everyone I meet that I stay home, it will soon be common knowledge. The playgroup will be great for the girls and an easy way for Lisa and I to meet new people. I should be able to get a lot of neighborhood gossip from the group as I am sure they talk about me when I am not around. Knowing the way the gossip already was starting to fly around the room, I wouldn't pass it by that my story is on the internet for all the other mothers to read up on. That's ok, my manhood was questioned today but everyone there realized along with myself, I am 100 percent man and a damn good father. The only thing I might worry about the playgroup is with all the cakes and coffee that I am sure I will indulge in week after week, I might gain a few pounds. If that is the sacrifice I have to take for my daughters to enjoy themselves, then so be it. There will be just more of me to love.

Wednesday

I usually have one cup of coffee a day, no more, no less. Today I had to have two. Why? I was one of the thousands of other Star Wars freaks that went and saw the latest chapter of the saga at midnight. By the time I got home it was roughly 3 a.m. So I am chugging along today on only three and half hours sleep and I am paying for it. Luckily I called McKenzie's new best friend's mom and asked her if I could ship McKenzie over there to play. McKenzie has been asking to go over there since the playgroup meeting so I am not just trying to get rid of her because I am tired, she really wants to go. She went over there for three hours as I rested on the couch and took care of only one child. I remember when we just had McKenzie and how hard we thought we had it with one baby, but after having Josie, having one child is like a walk in the park. It is so easy having just one compared to having two or more. If I could go back in time and realize how good we had it with just McKenzie, I am sure I would have done things differently. With two you are a lot more tied down and structured than with just one. Although I am ready to pass out, I have been enjoying spending quality time alone with Josie as I very rarely ever have her alone without McKenzie around to butt in. The rest of today will just be to do whatever makes everyone happy since I don't have the energy to yell and hope I make it until nap time. Not only their nap time but mine as well. I am sure I will make it since "the force is with me."

Thursday

One of my best friends from home, who actually is Josie's godfather, is coming into town for five days. McKenzie is very excited, as am I. McKenzie will have someone else to bother and play with all day besides me. I also know we will hit the golf course a couple of times before he departs for home. He will be a witness of my hard work and sweat as he will be home with me during the day as I take care of my girls. He doesn't know it yet, but he will be doing most of the playing as I will be doing most of the watching. It will be perfectly fine with him; he loves my girls and they love him. Many people questioned my decision on having my friend as the godfather for Josie rather than the usual pick of a family member. I chose him because I know if anything ever happened to me or Lisa, I would be able to rest in peace knowing that they are in good hands with him. Lisa and I are considering changing our will to make it legal that my friend would get legal custody of my children if something ever happened to Lisa and I. That is how much we care and love my friend. We haven't really discussed it seriously with him, or between ourselves, but I would bet the farm there would be no arguments coming from him on raising our children. Friends like him only come around once in awhile, so when they do, grab and hold on to them as they may become some of the most important people in your lifetime and your children's. Excuse me now, I have to make a tee time.

Week 34
May 24th-28th

Tuesday

My friend left today after his five day visit as Josie decided that it is time for her to walk. Josie for the past couple of weeks flirted with walking, as she would let go and take a few steps before plopping on her butt. Not now, she darts across the room like a drunken chicken crossing the road. She had to show off for my friend that she can walk as Lisa and I just sat there shaking our heads as we knew all along Josie could walk, but had to wait for her to let us know she could. Now with Josie able to walk, another chapter has closed with another chapter opening. Josie is growing every day as her tenure of being a baby is practically over. If Lisa and I do decide we are not going to have anymore children, we have just gone through our last days of being parents of a baby. Josie is no longer a baby, she is a toddler now as she struts through the house smiling and giggling showing off her walk and her four teeth. It is sadness and joy at the same time as Josie progresses into being a beautiful little girl just like her big sister. They are growing up way too fast, but there is nothing we can do about it. My parents have gone through it, Lisa's parents, and in the future my girls will experience the joy of being a parent and watching their babies grow up in front of their eyes. As much as I don't want them to grow, they still do. As McKenzie will be three years old next week, it feels like three months. I feel sorry for the parents who abandoned their children or have to give them up for adoption because the past three years of being a father have been the best three years of my life. They even beat my college years by tenfold, I realize now I didn't know what life was truly about, as now I do, I am a proud father of two beautiful wonderful daughters.

Thursday

With Josie walking and falling all over the place now, my life is a little bit more hectic. Every time there is a bump followed by a scream, I have to go running to see if there are any broken bones or any blood spewing out of Josie's body. Josie has really turned it up a notch as she now is really into everything as she is able to stand and walk to her destination. She has also come up with a screech that could peel off a fresh coat of paint. If something doesn't go her way, or if there is something she wants, she just rips off a screech that would make any alien run for his life. She is unbelievably loud and obnoxious. I am somewhat embarrassed when she does it in public because she sounds like a spoiled, selfish little brat. Lisa states we just have to work on her getting to talk when Josie wants something instead of us giving into her when she begins to scream like a siren. It sounds like the logical thing to do but when her siren goes off, I throw everything I can at her to shut her up. Lisa gets mad at me since I don't have much patience with Josie, but I just can't handle it sometimes. My mother told me I was the same way. Since I was the baby of three children, all I had to do was point and scream, thus creating a stir from my brother and sister to give me anything I wanted. They didn't want to hear me scream and cry much like I don't want to hear Josie. Problem with this solution is I didn't talk until I was three years old and we want Josie to talk sooner than that. This means I will have to work with Josie to talk instead of her pointing and screaming that she has come accustomed. It will be hard for both of us as her method has worked to this point, and I will have to learn to have more patience and not give into her demands without her trying to speak. I did show real big patience today while I was giving the girls their baths. Today being Thursday it was bath day. Giving the girls their baths always take a lot of patience and willingness as they splash and kick, which results in myself getting a bath wanting one or not. I have learned that when I do give them a bath, I am only in shorts as I quickly get covered in water. As I placed them both in the tub, I went into their rooms to get their clothes that they will be put in once they are finished in the tub. During this time, one of the girls must of farted and let out a little more than they wanted, because when I arrived back into the bathroom, the water and the girls were covered with little brown floaties. I couldn't tell which one did it as I investigated, but I am glad they did it in the water and not in their pants or on the carpet. Now I have a bathtub full of bubbles, toys and brown smelly floaties. So I quickly bathed them and got them out of the tub as fast as I could. I didn't get upset or frantic, I just thought of Bill Murray in *Caddyshack* when he found the Baby Ruth bar in the pool, picked it up and took a bite and told everyone, "It's ok, it's not that bad." It had to be the fastest bath the girls every took as some of the floaties grabbed onto my arms like leaches as all I can do is spray them off as I hurried to get the girls out. After the girls were cleaned and dressed, all I can say to myself was, "Oh well, shit happens."

Monday

Today is Memorial Day which means Daddy gets a three day weekend. Even though I don't go into the office anymore, holidays are the same for me as Mommy gets to stay home instead of going to work. McKenzie gets very excited when Mommy tells her that she is going to be home an extra day from the weekend. I am just as excited, as I am able to do other things around the house as Mommy entertains the girls. The perfect world would be if neither of us had to work and we both stayed home with the girls. Since we don't live in a perfect world and things in this world cost money, one of us has to work until we receive that letter in the mail that a very rich uncle we never knew we had, has passed away and has left us his entire fortune. I would just smile, as I would head for the golf course and Lisa to the mall. Life would be good, real good. Even though that day may never come, life is still pretty damn good.

Tuesday

The girls and I went to playgroup today, our third overall. It was great for the girls, but a little boring for me. McKenzie has a blast and looks forward to going every week, as am I for different reasons. McKenzie likes to go so she can play with all her new friends, I like to go to listen to all the women gossip. Once I arrived I did my usual routine, I let loose McKenzie and Josie and I nestled into a corner to sit back to watch the kids and listen to the women. This is better than *Oprah*. The usual topics came up; schools, children, complaints about the builders of our homes, and other usual babble. No good gossip or mud flinging was going on so I was getting a little bored. I went into the kitchen; fixed myself up a cup of coffee as Josie and I ate three or four slices of pound cake. I really didn't say much, I just like to listen, although I did make one comment. Some of the kids snuck upstairs while everyone was talking and began jumping on a bed making a lot of noise. This did not go over well with the mother hosting the playgroup as she rushed upstairs to stop the madness. One of the women commented on how her husband was watching their kids and he let them jump on their bed to keep them occupied. So I had to burst out and ask, "What does that mean?"

Meaning men let their children do whatever and the women would never let such a thing happen. A few women laughed, but the one that made the comment tried to back track what she said, but it was too late, I busted her. A neighbor on our block had to leave early because she was having work done at her house so I told her I will bring her son home since he was having a good time with the other kids. McKenzie really likes her son; he could possibly be her new best friend. It is weird, I don't know if it is just coincidence or not, but some of McKenzie's best friends are boys, not girls. She did however have a friend back home she really liked and she was a girl one-year-older than her. She still brings her name up so she likes girls too, so I shouldn't have too much to worry about in the future, I hope. When I was growing up I always wanted my best friend to be a girl. I don't know why, but I just did. The block we grew up on had nothing but boys so I never got that chance. By the time I grew up and knew some other girls my age, I didn't want to be their friend, I wanted to date them. So maybe McKenzie will have that opportunity to have her best friend to be of the opposite sex. The playgroup itself was very good as it lasted almost three hours as I had to pry McKenzie and her friend off the swing-set and drag them home. Before we all left, I had been meaning to ask the women what gets the red clay out of clothes. We have never experienced having to clean red clay out of our clothes since we are from the mid-west and all we have is black dirt. We already have five out of six items of clothing that Lisa cannot get the red clay out. I had to ask someone before we go broke down and bought new cloths every time the red clay ruins an outfit. I figured someone had to know how being around the red clay a lot longer than us. I was a very hesitant to ask, I waited until there was only four women left and I didn't want to sound so domesticated. I have to keep as much of my manhood that I have left, but I felt this was very important information I must have so I finally blurted out "what magic potion gets out this red clay out of cloths?" Without hesitation one of the women simply stated dishwashing soap. No shit, dishwashing soap. Lisa has been soaking and scrubbing trying to get this red menace out of our cloths and the solution is simply dishwashing soap. I went home and put her method to the test as McKenzie's outfit she wore was covered in red clay. As I scrubbed it with dishwashing soap I thought to myself it can't be this easy and simple? It was, the red menace was gone like a dog in heat. Even though the playgroup didn't feed me with any good neighborhood gossip, it did inform me on how to keep our wardrobes red free. Next week I will try to find out where I can go to buy beer at a reasonable price. Since we now live in the Bible Belt, alcohol is a sin, and I am a sinner going broke!

Friday

I received a call from my mom today stating they are coming down for a visit next week. My mom and dad were supposed to go on an Alaskan cruise during this time but the doctors recommended my mother not go in her current condition. She is not doing very well. She is discouraged as my dad seems not to be. I think my dad and I have the same theory in life; "If you ignore the problem, it will go away." My dad and I both realize my mother's illness will not go away without a miracle from God. I am both excited and weary at the same time as my mother comes to visit. Very excited for the girls as they love their grandma and grandpa. My parents are also bring two of my sisters kids with them which will be good for McKenzie. On the other hand, I am not looking forward to seeing my mom in her condition. It will break my heart seeing the mother I love so much practically dying in front of my eyes. I will do the best I can not show my emotions of hurt, but try to make this visit the best possible as I pray there are many more to follow.

Week 36
June 7th-11th

Tuesday

Just like State Farm Insurance, "Like a good neighbor," I invited McKenzie's new friend over for lunch. I figured for two hours or so I would get the real feel of what it would be like to have three children and would I really feel like killing myself by the time it was over. I wasn't too worried though, the boy McKenzie is friends with is pretty well behaved and they seem to get along, as she has been over to his house a couple of times already and she hasn't come home with any broken bones or cracked teeth. He was very excited to come into the house as was McKenzie . Immediately, like a good host, McKenzie showed him around the whole house including her bedroom. I don't know if I like the fact that boys are already visiting her bedroom, but at age four I am not going to worry just yet. Poor little Josie tried to keep up with them but couldn't. It was funny watching her chase her big sister around, but the two of them ignored her like she wasn't even there. I am sure this is just the beginning of the little sister trying to hang out with the big sister and big sister not wanting her little sister around. Josie will just have to get friends of her own which I am sure she will. I was a little worried that he would get bored at our house since it is not filled with power rangers or army men, instead we have plenty of dolls and a kitchen set for them to play with. But to my surprise he did have fun playing with one of McKenzie's dolls as McKenzie seemed to get a little jealous. I had to explain to her how to share, since she is very emotionally attached to her dolls as it is like pulling teeth to get her to share them even with her own sister. She did well though as she let him play with the doll. I think he got attached to the doll because it is a boy doll. I fixed them both lunch as they sat togther on her toy picnic table in the family room. I fixed them both the exact same lunch so there wouldn't be anything to fight over. They didn't finish their lunch, as they just wanted to just play together. Josie still wanted to be part of their fun but they ignored her still. The last half-hour or so we went outside as I started to get tired. I needed to waste time before I was able to bring McKenzie's friend back home. The house was a disaster as I didn't even hear the tornado sirens go off before the tornado hit. Finally it was time for everyone to take a nap, especially me. I put all the kids in our wagon and dropped off our neighbor safe and sound in one piece. It really wasn't too much trouble as they both entertained each other as I tried to keep Josie out of their way. As I pick up the pieces of what is left to my house, I think to myself that two is a hand full and three must be just chaos. I need to go to sleep now, goodnight.

Wednesday

Josie has gone from one of the best eating babies I have known to one of the worst. I don't know what happened? We used to give Josie anything and she would eat it, not now. She is now completely off baby food, not to our doing but from hers. She doesn't want anything to do with it. If I try to give her a jar of baby food, she will turn her head back and forth not allowing me to get the spoon in her mouth. Sometimes I think her head spins all the way around like Linda Blair's did in the *Exorcist*. Then if I do happen to get some baby food in her mouth, it comes right out, again like Linda Blair in the *Exorcist*. It is so frustrating trying to feed her now since I don't know what to give her. I had at least eight jars of baby food left that Josie will not eat. I gave them to our neighbor so they wouldn't go to waste. She eats a bowl of oatmeal now for Lisa at breakfast. Maybe that is filling her up for lunch because she is not eating anything I give her. She drinks all of her milk, which makes me fell a lot better. At least I know she is getting some nutrition. I tried to give her mini raviolis today; she wouldn't have anything to do with them. I tried her favorite crackers; she whipped them at me. I tried yogurt, spit it out at me. As my temperature rose to 105, I calmly just gave her a piece of cheese and she finally ate that. The cheese only lasted 5 minutes so what now? I know she is still hungry but everything I give her she either throws it at me or spits it out. I walked around the kitchen and went to the old favorite of most kids, cereal. I gave her a hand full of Corn Pops and she went to town. Finally, something that she will eat. Now that she is eating it is time for Daddy to eat. My lunches have improved since I started staying home. My lunches when I worked consisted of a microwave dinner or a sandwich. I only like two types of lunch meat, ham and turkey so there wasn't too much to choose from there. Now that I am home, I get to choose from whatever I can make out of the refrigerator. My wife is so jealous of my lunches since she is still eating the same old things over and over like I used to. I make myself grilled hamburgers and hotdogs, grilled cheese, oven baked pizzas, hot sandwiches, etc, etc. I feel like I am going out to lunch everyday at the office, but I am having it in the convenience of my own home. Even though Josie is having a rough time right now about what she wants to eat but I am not. Another bonus is if I ran out of food at work, I sat there hungry, not the case at home. If I am still hungry I just have to go back into the kitchen and fix me some more eats. I feel bad when my wife takes a peanut butter and jelly sandwich to work and I end up making a tasty grilled hamburger with fries at home. I really don't but it's the thought that counts. Bon appetite!

Thursday

We put McKenzie in a gymnastics class for the summer to give her something to do. She really loved going to school so we decided this will keep her involved being in part of a group class. Her first class was last week, but Lisa took off work in the morning to take her so I did not go, meaning this will be my first week. The obvious concerns cross my mind as usual; how will Josie act without her morning nap, will I be the only man there and what will the women think of me; will McKenzie break her neck, etc, etc. We arrived on time and McKenzie was very excited. She looks so cute in her little one-piece spandex outfit. To my surprise there were four other men there besides me. I felt a lot more relaxed and comfortable. There were plenty of women as well, as we all had to sit outside of the gymnastics room looking through glass windows without any air conditioning. Yes it was hot, very hot. Then put in the mix about 10 other children under the age of three and you have yourself a madhouse. Josie just wanted to walk outside, so I really didn't get to watch McKenzie too much, but what I saw of her she seemed to really be enjoying it and was having a lot of fun. Once I was able to lasso Josie back inside by bribing her with licorice, I was able to watch McKenzie for the last few minutes. I also had something else to watch besides my daughter. Another woman, not being shy in front of men, decided to whip out her breast and feed her little baby. This has now happened to me twice in the past month. I believe breast-feeding is wonderful and the best thing a mother can do for their child. Lisa breast fed both our girls. I have no problems with public display of breast-feeding and women should be able to do it wherever and whenever they need be. It was different this time as the mother undressed herself to feed her child. I, being a man, had to take a peak. I know it is wrong but this mother was very attractive and I still have the instinct if there is an exposed breast, it is my duty as a man to take a peak. It wasn't a long viewing since I didn't want her noticing me noticing her. Like I said, it is one of the most beautiful natural acts a mother can do. Class was over as McKenzie came out of the room and was very excited. In a way, so was Daddy, I can't wait til next week. I'm sorry, but I am 100 percent male.

Week 37
June 14th-18th

Tuesday

The long weekend is over and the clean up after hurricane Major begins. For five days we had a houseful of guests. My mom, my dad, my mom's best friend from South Carolina, and two of my sister's kids. That with myself, Lisa, McKenzie and Josie, and a barking dog, makes for a very long weekend. It was a very good visit even though it was total chaos most of the time. Lisa and I did everything in our power to make everyone happy, but sometimes that isn't good enough. I do get upset when things don't go my way, and when things don't go my way, I often express my feelings honestly, which means sometimes I should just bite my tongue and not say anything at all. So there were a couple of times that I had to calm down and not fly off the handle. I didn't want to do anything that would upset my mother. All things considered, she looked and acted pretty well. I was prepared for the worst for this being the first time I was going to see her in almost three months. From my phone conversations with her, she sounded like she was on death's door. Lisa and I both agreed she looked better than we thought she would.

Lisa and I have been having discussions lately about McKenzie's afternoon nap. Lisa thinks she doesn't needs her nap anymore. I have to explain to Lisa that if McKenzie doesn't get her nap, she turns into a child that no mother or father could love. Lisa would like to discontinue her nap, or at least shorten it, since McKenzie isn't going to bed til 9 pm. One of the reasons I give her a nap is so Lisa can spend time with her at night since she works all day. Instead of McKenzie going to bed at 7 pm and spending no time with her at all, she is now able to spend a few hours at night before McKenzie goes to sleep. The main reason why McKenzie needs a nap is she gets up I believe very early for most kids. She is up in the morning with her mom by 6:30 am. I hear from other parents that their children don't get up til 8 or 9 am, which I could see why there would be no reason for them to take a nap. But getting up at 6:30am makes for a long day for anyone, especially a three year old, so I believe she needs her nap. Lisa got a taste of her own medicine during the weekend. With us having so many people over, McKenzie was too pumped up to take a nap one day as we tried to get her down, but couldn't. We paid for our mistake twofold. Long before it was time for her to go to bed for the night, she turned into Satan. She was whiney, mean, crabby, unruly and just unbearable to be around. She went from a precious little girl to the "Devil." The only good thing that came out of it was my proof to Lisa why I still give McKenzie her nap. She agreed that she needs her nap and will not doubt me anymore. Lisa thought that I was giving her a nap for my selfish reasons, but that is not the case. I will admit I like her nap time since it gives me alone time, but without her nap, she does turn into Rosemary's Baby. So I am off the hook for awhile with McKenzie's nap schedule. I am glad Lisa was able to experience McKenzie without her nap for herself. She often doesn't believe me when I try to explain how the girls act. She thinks I exaggerate things out of proportion since her girls can be nothing but angels. I might exaggerate on occasions, but that is how I have to drive a point across to someone who doesn't experience it first hand. It bothers Lisa when I know the girls a little better then she does. She won't admit I do, but we both know it. It is just natural since I am the one home all day with them and know their schedule and how they react to certain things. Even though I find raising my girls easy and enjoyable, someone who isn't with them all the time finds it difficult. I hear it all the time from the mothers in the playgroup on how when their husbands watch the kids for just a couple of hours on the weekends, when it is all over they comment, "How do you do this all day, everyday?" It takes patience and the will to succeed just like anything else. It maybe the hardest job in the world, but also the greatest!

Thursday

The name game. I always made fun of my mom and dad when they couldn't get my name right. I would be called my brother's name; my sister's name, my dad's name, and even the dog's name before mine. I would always comment, "You don't you even know my name!" Well, I catch myself doing the same thing. I see Josie walking around the kitchen sucking on a 9 volt battery or the wood glue she has taken out of one of the drawers, I yell out McKenzie's name, then Brodie's name, before finally thinking who I am intending to yell at and finally get out the correct name. It is amazing how you are looking at one child and still be able to call out the wrong name. It's even more difficult in my situation since all three of my culprits I need to speak at all have names that rhyme. McKenzie, Josie, Brodie all end in "ie." This was completely by accident. We really didn't realize this phenomenon until after we named Josie that all our offspring have "ie" at the end of their names. Also, all three are girls. Could this be an episode for the x-files? Probably not, but it is weird how this all turned out without us even thinking of it or planning it this way. It is cute, but also confusing. We originally were going to name Josie, Madison, but we figured McKenzie and Madison were very similar, making it difficult. That theory does prove itself, but names don't have to be close to make the mistake. My mom and dad did it all the time and our names are Mark, Michael, Kim and Carl. Relatively close but not exact. I guess the more you have, and the older you get, you just scream out whatever name comes out first go down the list until eventually you'll get it right.

Week 38
June 21st-25th

Monday

I believe McKenzie is old beyond her years. Granted she is only three years old, but sometimes she acts like she is 33. She is a very emotional, caring child. She is always concerned about other people's feelings, especially other little boys and girls. If she hears a baby crying in a store or a restaurant, she will ask her mom or me, "Why is that little baby crying?" We have to answer some sort of reason such as, "The baby is hungry or tired." After we answer her, McKenzie demands that we feed the baby or put the baby "night night." Other instances is she will cry during sad moments during a video. She cried when she watched *Lady and the Tramp* when Lady was put into the kennel. She got very upset and emotional and wanted Lady out right away because Lady was sad and crying. It is amazing how she can grasp all of what may be going on in a situation and have emotions towards the situation. At night I dictate what is on the television so it is very rare that she watches any televison after 5 pm. I was watching a situation comedy in which during it a woman gave birth. After the woman delivered the baby, McKenzie started to cry. McKenzie was so into the woman's feelings and emotions they carried over to her. Lisa and I just looked at each other in amazement on how McKenzie picked up what was going on on the television show. I don't know if most kids are like this, but she is very in tune to her surroundings and is a very emotional, caring little girl.

On the flip side, she also can turn into a little brat. She doesn't turn into a brat often, but when she does it isn't very pretty. I always get a kick out of parents when their child acts up in front of other people and how quick they are to defend their child. "Oh he or she is just tired," or "I don't know what got into him or her, they never act this way." Just face it, your kid is being a brat. I am the first to admit it when McKenzie acts up and is being a brat. I do not try to defend her by making up some lame excuse of why she is acting the way she is. As it turns out; it is always the same parents with the same kids that are always tired or hungry. Imagine that, what are the odds? They don't want to correct the problem, so be it, I don't have to live with it. I won't live with a brat and my children know it. Whenever McKenzie decides she is not going to listen and have her little screaming fits, I let her know right there and then, she better knock it off and turn into the beautiful little girl I know and

110

love, or else! Granted sometimes it takes awhile before McKenzie gets back to earth, sometimes not until her mother comes home, but at least I don't let her get away with it and she knows she has been bad. I don't have much patience with her when she becomes a brat. It isn't my fault, it is hers. She is so good all the time, so when she does act up, I can't take much of it. If she was a brat all the time, I am sure I would be immune to it, but she isn't so when she is bad, it's bad. McKenzie knows when to stop; I push all the right buttons. I threaten her with all the stuff she loves which gets her attention. I will tell her I will take away her baby dolls, her swing set and lately the swimming pool. The swimming pool is a big bargaining chip since she loves going swimming. All I have to do is threaten her that she will not go swimming for a week and she stops misbehaving in a flash. Kids are wonderful to be around when they are good, but they are awful to be around when they are bad. So far I have been blessed with a very good girl with McKenzie. I have a bad feeling about Josie, real bad, but that only time will tell. God, have mercy on me, please.

Wednesday

I am starting to handle it a lot better, but it still makes me very uneasy and nauseous. The deed that I hate most in life; cleaning throw-up. This is now the second time since I have been staying home that McKenzie has decided to test my dedication to her by throwing up. It started when she woke up this morning with an upset stomach. Lisa and I have learned that she doesn't lie for attention, so we told her to just lie on the couch and drink some water. Lisa left for work and I had a couple of errands to run close to home so I didn't think much of it. She just laid back in her car seat as she turned greener by the mile. I thought to myself this was not a good idea and visioned myself cleaning out the van full of kid barf. That started to make me sick so I pressed on the gas pedal and hurried home as fast as I could. As I pulled into the driveway, I wiped the sweat from my brow from relief that McKenzie was able to hold it in. I pulled McKenzie out of the van as she walked inside the garage. As I reached over to get Josie out, I heard a splash on the concrete that I haven't heard since my college days. I didn't even have to look, I knew McKenzic has just unleashed her beast inside the garage. I put Josie back in her seat as I peaked inside to see McKenzie standing still in a puddle of her throw-up. The smell hit me like a heavyweight boxer as I did everything in my power not to loose my breakfast. I cannot help myself, something with the smell and sight of throw-up makes me weaker than a fly. I thank God McKenzie was able to hold it in until we reached home rather than her exploding in the van. I stripped her naked inside the garage, grabbed the

111

garden hose and rinsed off my garage floor and my daughter at the same time. She was very relieved, as was I, when all the "yuckies" were off her body as it headed down my driveway into the street towards the sewage drain where it belongs. At least I didn't have to touch any of it, as the hose did all the work. I got her dressed and gave her some 7-up to drink and me a beer as we lay on the couch together as I rubbed her stomach. Within no time she felt 100 percent. It could have been worse, so I should count my lucky stars this time that she unloaded on the garage floor rather than me or the van. You can give me the dirtiest diaper in the world and I'll change it without even flinching, but when there is throw-up involved, "Houston, we have a problem!"

Friday

Lisa was out in front of our house last night talking with a few neighbors as I did my best impression of Paul Bunyan cutting down some broken trees in our backyard. When we came inside she told me that one of neighbors, that is in the weekly playgroup, told her that I am just wonderful with my girls and she cannot believe how good of a job I do with them. She also stated that I probably handle it a lot better than she does. Hearing words like that from other people is evidence enough that Lisa and I are doing the right thing by me staying home. I could never make the money my wife does, and if I am able to ignore all the stereotypes and whispering that goes behind my back, and raise our daughters the way I want them raised, I have no doubts once again we made the right decision. It is very encouraging to hear feedback from other parents on how well I have adjusted to staying home full time. I know I can do it, Lisa knows I can do it, I just like the satisfaction of letting everyone else in the world know I can do it. I am sure there are plenty of people out there that don't agree with our situation, but guess what, I don't really give a dirty diaper what they think. I am the happiest I have been in a long time and the people who disagree must not have a life of their own that is full of joy and love as mine is. Anytime anyone wants to challenge me regarding my life as a stay at home dad, I would love to debate him or her on national television and tell the world exactly what I feel.

Week 39
June 28th-July 2nd

Tuesday

All weekend long I prepared for today. I don't know why I made such a big deal out of it, but I cleaned the house from top to bottom, went shopping for cakes and muffins, and Lisa made homemade fudge. Why? Today was the day that all my "lady friends" were coming over for the first time. It was my day to host the weekly playgroup. I shouldn't have gotten all bent out of shape about them coming over, but I just wanted my house to look good and for everyone to have a good time. I just had our playroom painted by an artist and it looks spectacular. The playroom sits right outside our main family room. Lisa and I decided to make that room the girls' playroom so we can watch TV as the girls play in the room next to us, this way we can keep an eye on them while we try to relax. The room is painted in a desert theme. The room is filled with rolling hills, cactuses, desert plants, mountains, animals and so forth. The best part of the room is in the middle of the main wall as you walk in is a mural of McKenzie and Josie holding hands as they stop to stare at a deer that is staring at them. It is so adorable you want to cry. Lisa loves it because there is enough room left on the wall to add more children. Anyways, I just wanted the house to look good and for the children to have a good time as I prepared for World War III, as I know as soon as they all get here, all the toys and games will be ripped into and thrown all over the place.

McKenzie was very excited that all her new friends were coming over to play with her, and for some stupid reason I was somewhat nervous. I shouldn't have been, but I was as I felt the pressure of being a good host. Within minutes, the house was full of people as the little patter of feet ran through the house, followed by screaming of excitement as all the children got together to play. For the next two hours, we sat in the family room talking, eating cakes and drinking coffee, as the kids tore up the house. The moms in the playgroup all have good kids as they all helped clean up the disaster before they went home. The two hours flew by like it was two minutes and we all had a very good time. My playgroup was a success as I was able to breath a sigh of relief when they all went home. It has been a task of mine to get McKenzie to play with all of the children in the playgroup, not just one or two. Since the playgroup had started, she really only played with the boy on our street. It's just she knows him the best, sees him the most, and

113

was really the first new friend she made after we moved. So it seems only natural that she would attach herself to him and shy away from the rest. I have stressed my voice explaining to her that it is better to have many friends rather that just one. For the past couple of weeks I have really worked hard and have gotten her to play with all of the children in the playgroup, and my work has paid off. She now plays with all, not just the boy, and when playgroup was over today, she wanted one of her new girlfriends to stay for lunch. I told her mother it was perfectly fine that she stays over for lunch. In fact I would prefer it to reassure my plan of getting McKenzie more friends. It took a little convincing from the girl's mom for her to stay. I don't know if she was just being polite to me since I have already had a lot of people over and was trying to get her daughter out of my hair, or she really didn't know me well enough yet to trust leaving her daughter behind for a couple of hours in my care. It is always hard to leave your child with someone new, but then add in that I am a man, not a woman, it might have been a little harder for her to do than normal. I insisted that she would be perfectly fine as I practically had to kick her out the door. One of the reasons she didn't want to leave her daughter behind was her father was leaving to go out of town and she wanted her to come home and spend time with him before he left. Then I think she realized that if she left her daughter with me during lunch, she would be home alone with him, all alone with him, before he left to go out of town. I think she realized this as she told me she would pick her up in an hour, when in fact she picked her up in two hours with a big smile on her face. Everything went fine for those two hours except it finally happened, I hit McKenzie.

The girls were very excited to play together as they ran around in joy. Once they entered the playroom, they would slam the door behind them. That is one of my biggest concerns, slamming the door. It tops my list of concerns as much if McKenzie is playing with a loaded gun. When I was in second grade, my brother and I were doing the same thing, messing around slamming doors in our bedroom when something terrible went wrong. I did not get my pinky finger out in time away from the hinges, as the door slammed shut it snipped off the top of my finger. There was blood everywhere, I was frantic screaming my head off as my dad rushed me to the hospital, while my mom followed with the remaining bits of my poor little pinky finger. To this day, I do not have a tip on my pinky finger and playing with doors brings a shiver down my back. If I could have it my way, I would take all the doors off in the house until my girls moved out. McKenzie and I have had several talks about the doors as once again I had to remind her that the doors do not get slammed shut. After we ate lunch, McKenzie's friend stated she had to go poopie. As she said that, the phone rang and it was a good friend of mine back home. I should of hung up and called him back but I didn't. So while I was talking to him, I was putting another person's child on the potty to go number two, I heard a horrifying scream, it was Josie. Her finger was being pinched like mine by my other daughter as she was shutting the bathroom door. Josie was hysterical as I dropped the phone from my ear to the floor as I opened the door to let her finger out, she was in horrific pain. I just hung up on my friend and without thinking I turned around and with the fingers of my hand, slapped down onto McKenzie's forehead. I was so mad, not only at McKenzie, but myself for being on the phone at such a critical time of the day. I had no business being on the phone as I took it out on my darling daughter. I blame myself 90 percent, but she knows not to shut the doors with Josie around. We just had this talk a little bit ago and the flashbacks of my own finger being lost by a door added to my anger. I held Josie until she calmed down as McKenzie hid and locked the door inside her playroom. Josie was still crying when I had to let her down to wipe her friends butt after she was done going to the bathroom. This is in the same category as a diaper. I don't mind changing smelly, dirty diapers when they are my own kids, but someone else's child, forget it. I feel the same way about wiping someone else's child's rear end, but you have to, it is part of the code of being a parent. Once I cleaned her up and Josie settled down, McKenzie and I had a heart to heart talk. I apologized profusely for hitting her. I explained that Daddy made a big boo boo by doing so and that I loved very, very much. I explained why I did it and promised her it would never happen again. I then explained to her the dangers of playing with the doors once again, but she just kept saying she was shutting the door so her friend could have some privacy. She was just trying to be a good friend and a good host and I hit her for it. Believe me, I felt like the gum on the bottom of somebody's shoe after that incident. Everything got back to normal as they began to play together once again. Josie seemed to recover from her near amputation and her little finger will be sore for a couple of days. I do regret hitting McKenzie, but it was just a reaction that I felt I had to do while protecting my other child. It was weird, since Josie is much smaller, it just seemed like that hitting McKenzie was the right thing to do since Josie couldn't defend herself. It was totally wrong of me to do so and I wish I had to whole thing to do over again so I could handle it differently. I believe I handled it fine, except for the hitting part. I just hope McKenzie's friend didn't see me hit her (I don't think she did as she was on the toilet at the time) because I don't want her going home and telling her mom what I did. One, she will never let her daughter come over and play with McKenzie again, and two I never hit her and I don't want her to think I am that way. She stayed another hour after the incident and wasn't afraid of me or asked why I hit McKenzie. I would think if she did see me, she would be afraid of me and would want to go home. I wouldn't blame her if she did. I would have to explain to all the mothers in the playgroup what had happened, as I know that the phone lines would be burning up and I might get expelled from the playgroup for being a child abuser. I hope this will not be the case. Her friend left with no other problems as McKenzie and I talked again and I apologized some more while we discussed the door situation. Everything is back to normal with our relationship as I kissed her forehead goodnight and told her how much I love her before she closed her eyes for her afternoon nap. Does anyone have any Valium?

Thursday

I have been trying very hard the past few weeks to get Josie to start talking. She is now 14 months old and doesn't say many words. Lisa and I agree that McKenzie at this age said many words, while Josie just grunts and moans. One would think the second child would have to speak even sooner to get their parents attention, but she doesn't care. When she is thirsty, she will walk up to the refrigerator, grab onto the handle, jump up and down while moaning the whole time. When she is hungry, she will walk up to her highchair and shake it. She is good in communicating to me what she wants, but will not do so by talking, just aggravation. Every time I know what she wants I will ask her questions. "Do you want you milk?" or "Do you want to come up on my lap?" hoping she would say yes or nod her head. Nothing. She will just stare at me until I give in. I don't have much patience with her because she knows I will give in sooner or later. It's not that I don't care, I do want her to talk, but it is just so frustrating because I know she can talk, but refuses. She is a very stubborn child, a martyr even. Lisa's whole side of the family are nothing but martyr's so I know where she gets it. The only words Josie says are "hi" and "da." She should be saying a lot more than she is, but she just won't. As much as it is annoying and frustrating, I must be more patient with myself and not let Josie manipulate me by giving into her without getting her to speak for what she wants. I am going to start putting the clamps down and get her to talk or otherwise she is going to be the only teenager to graduate high school by never speaking. That might be a good thing, if she never learns how to talk, she won't be able to talk to boys!

Friday

As Willie Nelson would say, *On the Road Again*. Tonight at 9 pm, we load up the van, the kids and my colon full of caffeine as we head out to the highway to make that 700 mile journey back home. We decided to go home with this weekend being a holiday giving us a couple extra days off. That is my wife has a couple of extra days off, I am off everyday. We have to drive back and forth for a couple more years until the kids get older. Once they are older, we will not have to bring so much junk when we travel. We have to bring the Pack N Play, a highchair, car seats, toys, clothes, diapers, etc and etc, which doesn't even include my stuff or Lisa's. If we were to travel by plane, I would have to charter my own 747 for all the stuff that goes along with having children. One full day of our short vacation is driving. Twelve hours there, twelve hours back. If this will not test our patience, nothing will. We probably won't drive back home again until Thanksgiving or possibly Christmas. We will have plenty of time to rest up until our next visit. I wish us luck and God speed.

Week 40
July 5th-9th

Wednesday

We pulled into our driveway this morning at 2 am. We just finished driving 1400 miles in five days with two small children across four states and lived to tell about it. Last Friday was no trouble at all. We left (as we did the first time) at 9 pm so the girls would sleep through the drive. They did as we made really good time back home. The weekend was surprisingly nice and relaxing. We were able to see all our family at a relaxed pace. There is nothing worse than driving 700 miles then getting in the van again to drive some more to see other people. Lisa's brother lives by himself and is about five minutes away from my parents house. We set up camp there since he lives alone and it is so depressing right now at my parents' house I wouldn't be able to handle it for five days. I visited my mother most of the weekend and she is not doing very well. I hate to say it, but it is just a matter of time and it is most likely for the better. Lisa's mom came down for a day to spend with the girls, as I went golfing. On the Fourth of July, it was really the first time McKenzie watched and understood fireworks. The first few she was a little scared, then after awhile she got used to them and enjoyed them. Josie clamped on tight to my shoulder blades but never cried. I was dreading the van ride back home, since I actually had a good time. The way back wasn't as smooth as driving in. With Lisa having to work the next day, we had to leave at a decent enough hour for Lisa to get some sort of sleep before going to work. We left at noon with this in mind. I knew the girls wouldn't sleep the whole time, which would result in some tense moments. All in all I can't complain on the ride back either. There was one time in which we just stopped for gas and a bathroom break in which we all went, even McKenzie, but five minutes back on the highway she decided she had to go poopie. Of course I lost my temper as we were just on the potty, and now we have to get off the highway again so she can drop off her baggage. I thought for a minute; which is better, getting off the highway so she can go, or getting off the highway to clean up the mess she would make if she dropped in her pants? As soon as that thought raced through my mind I took the first exit and pulled into a gas station so McKenzie could relieve herself. We pulled into our driveway at 2 am as we carried the girls to their beds as we thanked the lord for another safe and uneventful trip. It's too bad Lisa had to get up in four hours to go to work as me and the girls slept in to 10 am. That's a shame!

Friday

Sometimes I would just love to go up to people and yell in their face, "Leave my children alone!" This goes especially true for older people. Nothing against them but they are always in my children's faces admiring them. If you look at old people closely, they have to be scary in the minds of small children. They're wrinkly, overweight, loud and they have hair extruding from all parts of their bodies. This has to be just frightening to small children; especially babies like my Josie. I had a doctor's appointment today for my allergies. I wanted this to go as smooth as possible and I know bringing two children with me would be a task. I was able to drop McKenzie off at a neighbors house so I took Josie with me. At least I cut my aggravation in half. Everything was going fine; I registered with the nurse, filled out all my insurance information, then settled into the waiting room which they told me would be five minutes before the doctor would be ready to see me. Josie was being perfect as she looked around until a grandpa had to disturb her. This old man was probably 70 years old and had a big potbelly and more wrinkles than a Chinese Shar-Pei. He then decided to tickle my little Josie. I know he is just a sweet old man but please leave my child alone. I didn't say anything, but I wanted to scream. Well, he did manage to scare the diaper off her so she backed away, fell down, hit her chin on the chair, which resulted in an instant rage. Everything was going very smoothly and now I have a very upset little girl and I still need to see the doctor. This wasn't the end of the old man's interference either. Now he thinks he can calm her down by comforting her. Duh, you're the reason why she is bawling her eyes out. Finally I just had to pick up my baby and walk across the room away from grandpa. I wanted to beat him, but I really just wanted Josie to calm down as I was called in to see the doctor. I was able to calm her down as I bribed her with a piece of licorice. The rest of my doctor's visit went smooth as predicted without anymore interference for the old menace. It happens all the time. When are old people going to realize that just because I have cute and adorable children, they're not going to think that of them? Just like warning signs at the zoo, "Please don't feed the animals," I need to put signs on my children, "Please stay away or else!"

Monday

As I lay here on the couch poking my head up to look around the house to see if there is anything I should be doing, I feel kind of guilty. It's now 2 pm, my daughters are down for a three hour nap, the house is clean, all my chores are complete so all I really have to do is rest. Why do I feel guilty? My wife and the mother of my children is stuck in a cubicle or some useless business meeting and I have three hours to do whatever I feel like doing. I could take a nap, watch TV, talk on the phone, read, walk around naked, whatever I want. Not my wife, she needs to balance the company's balance sheet or something. Whatever it is, I wouldn't want to be doing it. I'd rather do what I am doing, nothing. That is why I feel guilty. How did I get so lucky that I am the one able to stay home and raise my daughters while my wife fights traffic and deadlines. Why is it me that gets to watch all my favorite reruns on televison while my wife stares at a computer all day. Why is it me that gets up at 6:30 am instead of my wife that gets up at 5:30am? Is it because I didn't land that dream job that makes me a lot of money? Is it because of instead of studying for a final in college I studied the bottom of a beer can? I don't know? These answers may never be answered, but I do believe this was my destiny. I feel bad sometimes that I have the life I have, but my wife seems very happy with her life so I don't dread on it too much. I do everything I can to make her life as good if not better than mine. She tells me all the time how great her life is and that makes me feel real good inside. It is hard not to feel guilty as she should be the one staying home with the girls, not I. I cannot turn back time to change things, but if I could, I probably wouldn't. Why should I? I am happy, Lisa is happy, and most importantly the girls are happy. Instead of feeling guilty I need to realize this is what life has chosen for me and accept it for what it is. What is it? It's pretty damn good!

Thursday

My heart was racing; my palms wet with sweat as adrenalin rushed throughout my body. This not only happened once this week, but twice. For only moments, which seemed like hours, I felt what it would be like to have a missing child. This first happened on Tuesday during our weekly playgroup. The playgroup this week was outside at a nearby park. It is a very large park with three or four playgrounds to choose from. The playground we were at was empty besides our group and a handful of other people. McKenzie was off playing at the top of the play set as Josie began to roam. Somehow I got distracted as I no longer could see Josie or hear her sweet voice. Panic struck as my worst fears rushed through my mind. Someone took my baby! Lisa and I both agree our worst fear in life would be if someone kidnaped one of our children. As horrible as it may sound, I would rather have my children dead than kidnaped. I couldn't live with myself knowing that my child is out there with some stranger, not knowing what is happening to her. The fear she would go through, as her wonderful life would be over as she knows it. We would have to live the rest of our lives wondering, searching, and longing for our daughter to come home. Our life would be over as it would never be the same again. My heart goes out to any living being who had to endure a lost child. As I began to panic searching for Josie those thoughts quickly raced through my brain. She was only missing for seconds, but it seemed to be an eternity. She was on the other side of the slide trying to go up it as the slide blocked my view of seeing her. No one else in the group noticed what happened except for me. One would figure I learned my lesson about not keeping a better eye on my children, then again maybe not. This time me and the girls were outside playing in front of our house as I decided since we are all out here I would cut the grass. The girls could keep playing and I could get some work done at the same time. McKenzie and Josie love being in front as they have all there toys in the garage as they pull them all out to play with. I can see them playing, but I cannot hear them with the lawnmower blaring. All of a sudden I look as I make my way back towards the garage without the sight of McKenzie. I see Josie, but no McKenzie. That horrible feeling starts up all over again as I rush into the garage to find her. I run in the back as she may have gone to play on her play set, but to no avail. I look down the block, nothing. This time it is longer than a few seconds, it is now about a minute without me finding my baby. Where is she? The last time I saw her was in the garage and I never saw her come out. Where is she? I stopped, thought about it, then went inside the house. My baby was on the toilet going poopie. She was done going as she spoke telling me she just sat here waiting for me to wipe her. I couldn't wait to wipe her little butt as I hugged her like I haven't seen her in a year. I would have to commit myself to an insane asylum if I ever lost one of my babies. I don't know how people go on living whom have to live through the nightmare of losing a child to kidnaping. Unfortunately we live it a very dangerous world where kids are kidnaped all the time. It is horrible to say but you cannot trust anyone anymore, it is just too risky. This week was a wake up call for me that I need to keep both eyes on them all of the time. I am their guardian, their keeper, and their father. It is up to me and only me to protect them from evil. I will never let them down as long as I am alive, I promise.

Friday

"My 41st week is now complete,
Staying home the kids is not for the timid, or the weak,

I am strong, body and mind,
As my kids test my patience with all kind,

We have moved on during this time,
To a new house and state,
Our long distance calls are only a minute for a dime,

I have eleven weeks left, then it will be one year,
Since I quit my job to stay home for laughs and cheers,

After one year, there will be two, three, four and five,
But if we have another child, I might not make it through it alive!"

Week 42
July 19th-23rd

Tuesday

I was able to spend some one on one time with Josie today as McKenzie was invited over to a neighbor's house. I look forward to spending time alone with Josie anytime I get the chance to, since it is very rare that I am able to with McKenzie around most of the time. Today I came to the conclusion that Josie is going to be nothing but trouble as she grows up. She is the "demon seed." She is exactly the opposite of her sister. McKenzie is the "golden child," Josie is the "devil child." It is just amazing how children growing up in the same house, with the same rules, with the same parents can grow up totally different. At any age, McKenzie would sit on anyone's lap for hours as long they would read books to her. I tried to do that today with Josie. I read one page before Josie decided she didn't want to hear anymore as she started ripping the pages out of the book. McKenzie was very interested in learning. About the same age Josie is now, McKenzie knew the different parts of her face. I tried teaching Josie the parts of her face this morning. That lasted about 30 seconds as she decided to bite me instead. McKenzie never went into cabinets, Josie does. McKenzie was very interested in the potty, Josie isn't. Josie is just a baby menace. She followed me into the bathroom as I began to relieve myself. She stood there smiling at me as I smiled back at her, then she reached over the toilet water and grabbed my stream of urine. "That's just great," I yelled as my urine sprayed all over Josie, the bathroom floor and me. McKenzie always walked up to our dog Brodie and would pet her nice on the head. Instead of doing the same, Josie grabs Brodie's leash and whips the poor dog with it. McKenzie was speaking many words by now as Josie doesn't talk, not a word. Whenever she wants something she just screams as load as she can until we can't take it anymore and give into her demands. Granted we don't spend enough quality time with Josie as we did with McKenzie, but when McKenzie was growing up, Lisa and I both worked so I believe we actually spend more quantity time with Josie than we ever did with McKenzie, but not quality time. Even so, Josie continues to become more destructive and more unruly than a wild pack of dogs. She will put me in the grave at an early age, as I watch her decide to dump her bowl of macaroni and cheese on top of her head. What goes through this child's mind? There are a couple of qualities I do like thus far from Josie. She is much tougher than McKenzie as I am able to fight a little rougher and a little longer with her than I can with McKenzie. I usually will make McKenzie cry, but not Josie, she holds her own very well for being 15 months old. Josie also looks like she will be a good athlete. She can already through a ball as good as McKenzie. Josie gets good practice throwing as she is constantly throwing her food or milk cup. At least if she becomes an athlete, she would be able to afford her own bail money and not rely on us. Our McKenzie is as close to a perfect child as you can get. On the other hand, Josie is such a little terror; my words really can't describe what I go through with her on a daily basis. As bad as this sounds, I love that "little devil" very much. All kids will be different no matter what you try to do. We must of gotten lucky with McKenzie and this is God's way of paying us back for an easy time. I wouldn't trade her in no matter how bad she acts, or how many times she makes my head explode. I know she loves me too, even though when I yell and scream at her, she just looks at me and laughs with that grin on her face, thinking inside her little brain of hers "too bad dad, I will do what I want!"

Thursday

I was sitting in between three women today during McKenzie's gymnastics class. All they did for the whole 45 minutes was complain, moan, and basically bitch about everything and anything. I just sat there listening to these women ramble on and on as I just wanted to stand up and slap each one of them. First they complained, how hard it is to have children. What world did these women come from, Neptune? Everyone knows how hard it is to have children, and if you don't know, then you're just plain stupid. Even people who don't have children knows it is very difficult to raise children. Maybe not as hard until they actually have them, but they know. That is why Lisa and I waited 5 years to have children until we were ready for the responsibility and commitment in having children. There are so many people out there that want children, but can't have them for medical reasons or so forth. Then you have the ignorant people in the world who are blessed to have children and all they do is complain. Nothing makes me angrier than people moaning and groaning about raising a family. Then the women got into a conversation about cars vs minivans. One woman wouldn't buy a minivan because she states that is admitting to herself that she is old. What does age have anything to do with owning a minivan. I have had this argument with other people before. As parents, you're not looking for style points when it comes to vehicles. You're looking for the most practical vehicle you can own, and as much as people don't want to admit it, a minivan is the best vehicle you can own when you have children. They have the most room in them, they are the easiest to get the children in and out, and they are relatively safe. Another big factor about minivans is the cost of them. They are far less expensive that the "yuppie sports utility vehicles." I can name at least 3 couples that went the "yuppie" route and bought a sports utility vehicle instead of a minivan, and they have regretted it. They now admit they should have bought a minivan. One couple we know did take our advice and bought a minivan even before their son was born. To do this day they thank us all the time as they absolutely love their minivan. People have to realize and accept the fact they have children now, deal with it. To all the people out there that don't buy a minivan, but a Honda Accord instead, you're pretty much an idiot. By buying the Honda, you might think you are holding onto your youth, but look in the back seat, you have a child's car seat in there! How cool do you look now? You don't even have room to pack the car to see grandma because the trunk is so small you are only able to get a few things in it. Now your baby can't have it's favorite things since you were too selfish to buy a minivan. I have plenty of room in my van and I love it. I might always have a van as it has become a lifesaver for Lisa and I with our children. There is no comparison when it comes to any other vehicle. A minivan is the only way to go.

The women are right about staying home with children all day, it is hard, very hard. I hope that no one thinks it isn't hard, because it is. The fact still remains that you don't have to make it harder on yourself as I think some people do. There are many factors that come into play when you are staying home. It takes guts, sweat, and the will to be the best parent you can be. I believe the most single factor it takes to be successful at being a "stay home parent" is that you have to be happy. If someone is not happy being at home, don't do it, go back to work. Staying home with children is not for everyone, and if you are not happy doing it, no one in the house will be happy. There is an old saying "if Mommy's not happy, no one is happy." That is a very true statement. I am very happy staying home and as a result, our whole family is happy. You can't kid yourself, or try to hide the fact that if you don't like staying home, it will eventually wear you down to the point that you might suffer a nervous breakdown. It is just amazing hearing these women complain how hard they have it. They just don't realize how good they have it. Everyone there has enough money and resources for them to afford to bring their children to gymnastics, when there are plenty of children at home that don't even have shoes. It is a shame that a lot of people in the world take what they have for granted when some families can't even take for granted if they are going to eat dinner or not. I look in the parking lot and see them driving brand new vehicles, but still complain because "little Johnny" got up a half-hour early today. Staying home with my kids has really opened my eyes on how lucky I am, and how good my life is. I can write a whole book on the subject of "brat parents," but that is not my intention. People need to look at the big picture. If they are blessed with the opportunity for them to stay at home and raise their children without the means of daycare, they are very blessed indeed. I know I am. As gymnastics class ended, and all the ungrateful mothers picked up their children and hustled them into their sports utility vehicles, I picked up my daughters, hugged them both and told them I love them very much. Then I drove out of the parking lot in my minivan proud as a peacock!

Week 43
July 26th-30th

Tuesday

"Why do my children act the way they do sometimes?" "Why does Josie seem like all she wants to do is get into trouble?" "Why is it McKenzie is so smart at such a young age?" These questions and many more that I have been asking myself may have finally been answered today, and I don't like the results. My children are part alien! It's true. The truth has finally been discovered in a very particular way. Josie was acting her usual "devil" self and McKenzie was putting together puzzles that are supposed to be to advanced for her, as the truth came out, literally. I smelled in the air the all so familiar aroma of a "stinky diaper" from Josie. I snagged her from behind, grabbed my basket of wipes and a fresh diaper to change her and stop her fumigation of the house. As I peeled back the velcro straps, my eyes began to blind me as it appeared in front of my face, Josie's diaper was filled with bright green poopie! Not a tint of green, or a greenish brown, but a solid bright green. It was green as a lime. I couldn't believe my eyes as I never saw anything like this before. She has had tints of green poopies from when she teethes, but nothing as bright and obvious as this. It could only mean one thing, alien. I then realized that Josie is in fact an alien. It comforted me a little bit to acknowledge the fact that she is an alien. This is why Josie is the way she is. Josie was put on this planet from high above for some sort of secret mission from outer space as she lives with us to complete her mission, whatever that may be. If her mission is to drive me crazy, her mission is almost complete. It was McKenzie's turn next to go to the bathroom as she jumped up on the toilet to do her business. As always, when she is done she calls me into the bathroom to wipe her. As I reached behind her to wipe her, I was blinded once again. Another green monster has appeared from inside one of my children! It was long, green and stinky! Both of my children are aliens, as the proof is in their poopie. I couldn't believe it. As the glow from the poop lightened up the bathroom, I quickly flushed it down as I didn't want McKenzie to realize I am now on to her, that she is in fact an alien like her sister. As I calmed down, and accepted the fact that my children are aliens, and they extract green poop from their butts, it hasn't changed a thing, I still love them very much, no matter what planet they may be from.

Friday

This week was not a good week for us as parents, and a very bad week for our children as children. It all started with McKenzie getting bit by a red ant. Red ants do attack and bite which can cause serious pain. The ant bite not only caused serious pain to McKenzie; it caused her to have a reaction. She broke out into a rash and had a slight fever. Lisa visited our new pediatrician for the first time because of McKenzie's condition. The doctor said she is fine as we breathed a sign of relief. We were to notify him if McKenzie was not 100 percent within the next couple of days. Next we have Josie as she decided to climb out of her stroller while we took a walk around the neighborhood. As Lisa and I were talking about other people homes and so forth, Josie decides to climb out and crack her head solid onto the concrete street. We both saw her climbing out at the same time, but as soon as we lunged to grab her it was too late; she flipped herself forward as she smacked the back of her head solid onto the ground. It sounded like someone dropped a rotten cantaloupe. Instant rage came from Josie's lungs as we walked home swiftly to check out the damage. She had a big scrape as she wouldn't let her grasp loose out of Lisa's arms. I right away thought to myself that she probably has a concussion. She began to get very pale and sleepy. We had to keep her awake in case she did in fact have a concussion as vomiting usually will occur a short time after the blow to the head. About 30 minutes after the fall, Lisa received a little present from Josie; she threw up all over her. Now my conclusion was correct, our baby has a concussion. With us being new to the area, as good parents as we believe we are, we have no clue where to bring our daughter for medical attention. Lisa pulled out all our new insurance paperwork as I scrambled through it to find information on our doctor and the medical institution. Lisa was just comforting Josie as she was still pale, but conscious. Lisa and I are now feeling as low as dirt thinking to ourselves how could we have let this happen? All we did was go on a harmless walk around the neighborhood, and now we can be facing a life or death situation. You just never know what the future may hold. It was our fault by not strapping Josie in her stroller knowing she is very capable of standing up and doing what she did. Now in the time of a crisis we have to sort through numerous handbooks to find out who we need to call. Finally Lisa was able to call a doctor on call as Josie threw up for the second time. As we waited for the doctor to call back, I got out the bible of children's books *What to Expect the First Year* and looked up head traumas. After reading the book and checking over Josie, it was my conclusion that she definitely had a concussion. After she threw up for the second time, she was beginning to act like her old self. Laughing, walking, causing trouble as Lisa and I sighed in relief. The doctor then called as we discussed her prognosis over the phone. He agreed she had a concussion, but didn't need to see her unless she throws up one more time. He gave us directions to the children's hospital and told us to wake her up every two hours to confirm she hasn't dropped into a coma. So every two hours I woke Josie and Lisa up (Lisa slept on the floor next to Josie's crib) and Josie was waking up without any problems. Our nerves began to calm down as the only bright spot out of this ordeal is we now know who to call and where to go in an emergency. I am sure we are not the only parents out there that didn't know where to go or who to call in an emergency. It is something that you hope you never have to do, but you almost always have to do it once in your life. Lisa and I promised each other that we are going to become better prepared for emergencies so if and when there is a next time, we will be able to handle it better. You don't plan for these things as you hope that you never have to go through an emergency, but with kids it is going to happen a lot. I myself visited the emergency room four times. I cracked my head open when I was five. My finger was cut off a few years later, my chin was cut open, and I had a concussion. With girls I hope my emergency room visits will be to a minimum, as I can imagine with two boys, the hospital would probably become a second home to most parents. There will be accidents with a lot of blood, or broken bones, and as parents, we are going to have to act calmly as our daughters are going to rely on us to take care of them. I am not looking forward to any of these times, but it comes with the territory of being parents. You need to take the good with the bad, and hope the good always out numbers the bad.

Week 44
August 2nd-6th

Monday

When you are a parent and have small children, you must be able to handle multiple tasks, usually all at one time. This holds very true while driving. When I drive with my daughters alone, I have to turn myself into "rubber man." As I drive I am constantly reaching in the back with my arms attending to their needs. This includes giving them their drinks, food, wiping their noses or tickling them to get them to stop crying. My arm is like a large rubber band as it stretches from one child to the next. What happens mostly is I will give them their cups to drink, and it never fails one of them is bound to drop it on the floor. Now I must hunt for the missing cup while holding onto the wheel watching the road and other vehicles so I don't go crashing into a K-mart. Driving gets very hectic at times, especially if we have been out too long, meaning the comfort zone has run out of time and my girls are ready to explode. The crying, kicking and screaming by my two girls is amplified while inside a vehicle. Once I have passed my limit as the girls start to get out of control, I then turn into "super race car driver." I do whatever it takes to calm the girls down so I can drive home as fast as humanly possible without getting any speeding tickets. I can only handle so much of girls in the car when they get restless. It's hard enough to concentrate on the road without children in the backseat. I have become a one arm, one-eyed driver. Half my body is in the front seat, the other half in the back accommodating the girls. It is a very important skill all parents need to learn when dealing with kids in the car. Race car drivers have it easy. They only have to deal driving as fast as they can around in a circle, while everybody in the pit crew does everything else. Not a "stay home parent." We not only have to battle the other drivers on the road, but also tend to the needs of our children all at the same time. It sometimes becomes very dangerous as I try to do both drive and tend to my kids. There have been plenty of times when I might have been looking in the back seat, or not driving with two hands on the wheel and have almost been in accidents. I am surprised my insurance rates haven't increased as my risk doubled once I turn into "rubber man."

130

Thursday

When I was growing up I was very shy. I have broken out of my shell the last 10 years or so as my wife constantly reminds me that sometimes I should crawl back into my shell as I might be too outgoing at times. McKenzie is very shy, then we have Josie. I need to figure out if Josie is very outgoing or if she is just a pig. No matter where we are, if some other child is eating, Josie will go up to that child, or the child's parent and demand she gets included. In a way it is embarrassing to me as if I don't feed her so she has to beg from other people to eat, but on the other hand it shows me Josie is outgoing and will go out of her way to get what she wants. McKenzie never went up to strangers the way Josie does. Josie is a beggar, and she usually gets what she is after. I act it out like Josie shouldn't be begging for food, but the other people don't seem to mind sharing so I let it go almost all of the time. The times I don't let Josie get what she is after if it is something I don't want her to eat. People don't realize that once you feed Josie a little, she comes back for more. When that happens it does become embarrassing to me, as I try to pull her away from the source, then Satan comes out as she demands to get fed. Like in zoos where there are signs, "Please don't feed the bears," I need to have my own sign made, "Please don't feed Josie." It's not like we don't feed the child either. Our baby bag is full of cookies, crackers, and pretzels, etc; she just can't stand other children enjoying themselves without her being included. Josie will be the one putting the gray hairs on my head, that is if I have any hair left as it slowly falls out watching my girls grow up.

Friday

I might be 32 years old, but I am still quick on my feet and able to stay calm in emergency situations. This morning I had an emergency situation. It wasn't with one of the girls; it was with my digestive system. The morning started out as normal as any other morning. We ate breakfast, got dressed, and kissed Mommy off to work to begin our day. I needed to go to the hardware store for some paint, so I loaded up the girls in the van and off we went. It is about a 15-minute ride to the hardware store being we are driving in the morning rush hour. McKenzie loves going to the hardware store because she always gets a sucker. At the checkout counter there is a basket of suckers the cashiers hands out to small children. I consider that a bonus. I love going to the hardware store and there aren't too many 3 year old girls that like to go, but if there are suckers involved it helps get their motivation going. We were in the hardware store for about 10 minutes when the feeling of discomfort

131

began to overcome me. My stomach tightened up as severe cramping comes from below. "Oh oh," I said to myself as I am miles from home and I am about to explode. I ran to the cashier, gave McKenzie her sucker, and rushed them into their car seats. McKenzie then realized something was wrong as she can see the grimace look on my face. "Nothing honey, just sit back because Daddy needs to hurry home," I kept saying. She kept asking, "Why?" It was hard for me reply fearing any sudden movement would unleash the beast. I broke all speed limits, darted in and out of cars as I put our lives in jeopardy. I couldn't help it, the pressure was building, the pain was growing and if I didn't get home as soon as I possibly could, it would get ugly real fast! About a mile away from home I thought to myself I wasn't going to make it. I am now driving at the front of the seat with my legs crossed shut as McKenzie keeps trying to talk to me as I ignore her the best I can. She can be ruthless in interrogation as she must know what is going on at all times. Even if I make it home in time, I still have to get the girls out of the van, into the house and make my way upstairs to my safe haven. How I am going to pull this off without me exploding first? Sweat begin to pour down my forehead as if I was in a rainstorm. Finally I pull into our driveway, slam the van into park, run around the van to unstrap the girls from their car seats, pick them both up at the same time, and throw them inside without any explanation. At this time I believe it is too late as I feel the exiting occurring before I am able to reach home base. I hold my breath one last time as I make my final lunge into the bathroom. I am able to strip off my cloths just in time before the "demon" exits my body as I am now sitting to avoid an embarrassing moment as I make it safe and sound. My body and mind sigh a giant relief that could be heard for miles. I thank God for blessing me and girls a safe ride home as I beat the clock. Going to the bathroom is a whole new ball game when you are at home with kids. You need to plan it around your schedule; otherwise you might end up in a compromising predicament as I just encountered.

Week 45
Aug 9th-12th

Monday

    There have been some serious discussions between Lisa and I the past few days about the possibility of having a third child. I can't believe it myself that I would actually even consider having another child, but I can honestly say that I am considering having another baby. If anyone had asked me a few months ago if I was going to have another child, my answer would have been an enthusiastic "no." If anyone would have asked Lisa the same question, she would answer without hesitation, "yes." The tide has turned a little bit, which is a little weird. I am the one leaning more towards having a third; as Lisa is leaning towards not having anymore children. Our discussions are serious as we are trying the come up the answer, do we or don't we have another child? We both have doubts as we both agree many factors come into play. Do we have enough money? Do we have enough time? What effect will a third child have on our marriage? What if we have twins? We have enough to worry about with two; do we want to worry about three? These are shared concerns we have together. Lisa has some concerns that are different than mine. If we decide to have another child, she will not be able to spend the time off she did with McKenzie and Josie. She had at least 12 weeks off with both of them, as she would only have 6-8 weeks off with the new baby. She breast-fed both of the girls, would she be able to breast feed the new baby? Before Lisa went back to work, both of the girls were sleeping through the night. The new baby will most likely still be getting up in the middle of the night. Her bonding with the new baby would be minimal, as how much time would she really have to spend with the baby? Lisa would have to spread herself pretty thin as she has two girls demanding her attention as soon as she walks in the door, a full time job and a husband who needs a lot of loving. There are more and more factors that come into play for the mother, especially one that works full time, that needs to be considered when deciding to have another child or not. My concerns are more generic than hers. I am happy with two perfectly healthy children, why risk going for three? Our family would then be an odd number consisting of 5. I really don't want Lisa going through another caesarean section as she was told she cannot deliver vaginally. Instead of moving on with our lives, we take another step back for a few years will be dedicated raising and nurturing an infant. All of these questions and concerns are easy to answer. The answer being no. Then there are the benefits of having a third child. Lisa loves to be pregnant for some insane reason. We love having kids. The possibility of having a boy interests me. I have really enjoyed being at home watching my girls grow and progress into little ladies. As our babies grow and bring us joy and love everyday, there are countless reasons why to have more children. Lisa and I are very organized people and do things very systematically. This is the reason why we have made the date of January 1, 2000, the day we decide either to have a third child, or simply to move on with our lives and don't look back. There will always be doubts in either discussion we decide to make. If we don't have anymore children, we will ask ourselves for the rest of our lives, "Should we have had another child?" Then again, if we do decide to have another child, when times are tough, and things don't seem to be going our way, we will debate, "Why did we decide to have another child? Everything was perfect with just two." We need to seriously decide together as parents, lovers, and friends on whether or not to have another offspring. No matter what decision we decide to make, we must never look back to second guess ourselves and just look to the future for whatever it may hold. To have or not to have, that is the question?

Friday

"Thank God it's Friday" never sounded better than it does today. This week was not a very good week for me personally as I turned into the type of parent that a family fears. I don't know what happened, but for the most of the week I was not only waking up on the wrong side of the bed, but a couple of days I woke up on the floor. It might have had something to do with the conversation I had with my mom on Sunday, or the lack of a conversation. I called her in the morning to see how she was doing, but she was asleep. So I called back later in the evening, but she was in too much pain to come to the phone. Too much pain to talk to her own son on the telephone. What the hell is that? I just hung up the phone as I went into a state of shock. The reality that my mother is dying must of took a toll on me as by Wednesday I lost control of my emotions. Everything the girls did I yelled my head off at them. Nothing they did was unusual or out of the normal, but for some reason my patience and tolerance did not exist. Ed McMahon could have come to my door, told me I just won the Publisher's Clearing House Sweepstakes and I would have slammed the door in his face. Not only would I have slammed the door in his face, I would of thrown eggs at his car as her pulled out of my driveway. That is what kind of mood I was in. I jumped all over Lisa on the phone every time she called. I didn't clean up the house, write in my journal, I just didn't care about anything, except yelling and being down right mean.

As hard as I tried, I couldn't get out of the desire to be mean. I got meaner and nastier as the day went by. I hated myself as I am sure my family did also. I am glad I didn't go out in public, as I am sure I would of lost my temper with the girls making a public nuisance and fool of myself. Whenever I see other parents yelling at their children in public, I take note and think to myself what a jerk. That is what I was this week, a jerk. Something just came over me as I looked in the mirror and told myself I must get out of this funk. I couldn't stand myself anymore, plus I wasn't having sex with my wife as she told me to get away from her as long as I have this bad attitude. I am fine now as whatever possessed my body has disappeared. I called my mom back and we were able to have a good conversation as she sounded pretty good. I guess there will be days that are good for her and days that are bad for her, just like me. The only difference is that I have plenty of days left in life, she does not. I pray to God that whatever took over my body and mind will not reappear ever again, as if it does, I may never have sex again.

Week 46
August 16th-20th

Monday

I took a walk early this morning around the neighborhood as I have seen plenty of mothers with either smiles on their faces or tears in their eyes. Today was the first day of school of the new school year. The mothers with tears in their eyes are the first timers. They are going through many emotions and fears as they let go of their beloved child out of the safety of their arms as they watch them climb onto the yellow school bus as it drives their child away. It has to be very difficult the first time seeing off your child that you have been with non-stop for five years or so, as you now put them in the hands of complete strangers to care for them. In this day and age, school isn't like it used to be. School used to be one of the safest places on earth, suddenly it has become one of the most dangerous. With the violence growing within our school systems, I don't know how Lisa and I are going to handle it when it becomes our turn to let McKenzie and Josie climb onto that school bus. The violence among school age children sickens my stomach whenever I hear of such a tragedy. My heart goes out to any parent who has had to suffer through any such nonsense. School systems really need to have zero tolerance among any children within their schools that may portray any traits that they may be a danger to the other children. It is very scary to think that such violence does exist, as there have been numerous occurrences around the country. This is why as parents we have to do our best raising our kids and stay in tune with them as they grow. We will always worry about our girls no matter how old they get. Seeing them off to school is just the beginning of many worried filled days ahead of us. If I need be, I will just become a bus driver so I can drive them to school. If I am still uptight, I will just have to get my teaching degree and become their teacher so I can still be with them all day as they go to school.

On the other hand, I saw plenty of other mothers with smiles on their faces. These are the veterans; they have been through the first years and are excited that their children are back in school to give them to opportunity to do other things. Some mothers go back to work part time. Others take the time to catch up on the many chores that may have eluded them while the kids were home on summer break. Summer break is the opposite for parents than that of children. Children look forward to summer, parents do not. In a way, stay home parents get a little of their life back as they are now able to do what they want while their kids are in school. When the children are at home, their life is dedicated to them. Now that they are in school they are able to do the things they wouldn't be able to do if their children were at home. I am looking forward to that time even though it is going to kill me letting go of them as they go to school. I might get a part time job, or a permanent tee time, or just kick back on the porch and watch the grass grow. I don't know what I will do, but I am sure I will have plenty to do when that time comes. I still have a couple of years before I become one of those bawling parents standing outside on the corner watching their child climb onto that bus. I just hope that too many don't see me cry like a baby. If we decide not to have anymore children, I will only have Josie to keep me from freaking out after seeing McKenzie off to school. Josie will have to be my rock and take care of me as I quiver like a frightened deer. Even though it will be very hard on Lisa and I emotionally, I am sure we will make it through the first school year. When they are both in school, Lisa has mentioned to me that she will come home for lunch a couple of times a week, and I am excited about that!

Monday-continued

Lisa came home from work today with some bad news. She needs to go out of town for four days for work, so being a "stay home dad" really takes on a whole new meaning this week. I have had the kids to myself for as long as two days, never three full days and nights. The next four days will be a very good indication to me if I have fully transformed into a "stay home parent." I am easily able to handle the routine from morning til the time Lisa comes home from work, but now I have them all to myself for 96 straight hours without any sort of break. I have made out my battle plan for the week, as I have told myself I will not be stuck inside this house for four straight days without other adult contact. Lisa left this morning as the girls and I headed to our weekly playgroup. That took up all of the morning as we arrived home just after 12 pm. After my girls get up from their afternoon nap, we will eat dinner and go to the neighborhood pool. That will kill an hour or so and more importantly tire them out. After we come home from the pool, they will receive their bath. By then it will be time for Josie to go "night night" as McKenzie will be going to bed shortly after her. Tomorrow I have planned to visit a brand new mall that just opened up with some of the mothers in our playgroup. We plan on going early in the morning and come back early in the afternoon in time for their naps. In the evening we will either go back to the pool, or just do something outside to tire them out some more. On Thursday, I have made plans with our friends from Chicago, who now live in Georgia, to hang out at their house. McKenzie and their son are about the same age, so they get along just fine. My battle plan is in place as the next three days I am on my own without any relief from my wife at night. When she told me about her business trip, I freaked out for a minute. There are days were I cannot wait for Lisa to get home and relieve me to get these kids off my back and out of my hair. I won't have that safety net this week as Lisa will not be coming home and I am on duty all day and all night. It is not a problem as long as you accept it and handle it. It is a lot like alcoholism; the first step to recovery is accepting you have a problem. I have accepted the fact that I have the kids for three straight days without any help and I am totally fine with it. Actually, I am sort of looking forward to it for a couple of reasons. One, to see and prove to myself I can do it entirely by myself without the relief of Lisa at night. Also, to truly bond with my girls as many times at night they are so involved with their mom, they often forget about Dad. I never put them to bed at nighttime as Lisa always does it. I want my girls to realize that they can count on Daddy day and night, as I tuck them into their beds and kiss them goodnight and tell them I love them. Don't get me wrong though. When Saturday comes, when Lisa is back in town, I won't be around as I already have made a Saturday morning tee time as I plan to be kid free for at least 6 hours as I chase that little white ball around six thousand yards of grass. Oh, how I love that game. Golf will be my sweet reward of three days and nights of loving my daughters. What a life I have, fore!

Tuesday

It's about 9:30 pm and both of my babies are asleep, as I am about to pass out from exhaustion. Athletes think they have it tough with twice a day practices, try taking care of a one year old and a three year old, non-stop for two straight days. It hasn't been all that bad as I am making a conscious effort to stay busy and to stay out of our house. After Lisa left yesterday on her business trip, the girls and I went to our weekly playgroup. We stayed longer than we should have but I didn't want to rush home. We ate lunch, cleaned up and I put them down for their afternoon naps. When they awoke, we had a quick dinner and off to the pool we went. This would be the first time I have ever ventured to the pool by myself with the girls. I was a little nervous. In the past few weeks, four children have drowned in local neighborhood pools. Our pool is not open unless there is a lifeguard on duty so at least I have the comfort of some back-up help if I need it. McKenzie loves the pool and would stay in it until her skin fell off, but Josie is another story. She hates the pool and would rather just sit in the stroller and eat crackers and drink her milk. It was like pulling teeth keeping her in the pool for at least fifteen minutes, but I did it. Eventually I couldn't take her whining anymore as I gave into her demands and strapped her in her stroller and gave her what she wanted, her crackers and milk. It was the perfect time to go to the pool because it was about the time everyone else in the neighborhood was sitting down to have dinner so I had the whole pool to myself. That was very encouraging as the lifeguard only had us to keep an eye on so I was assured. We stayed about an hour and we packed up our things and headed back to the house, not in the house, rather outside in the front to play. Nighttime is a good time to play outside as it is cooler and more of the neighbors come out as they get home from work and finish their dinner. As the girls played, I was able to talk to other adults and use my brain. Other adult contact is very important to me as if I don't get my fill; my brain begins to turn to mush. As the girls and I worked up a good sweat it was time for baths. I wasn't up for giving them a bath as I began to run out of steam, I decided to throw them in the shower with me as it would be faster than giving them a bath. Whenever I don't feel like giving them a bath I take them into the shower. They don't enjoy it as much of as the bath, but it is faster and that is what I was looking for at the moment. I was able to get them down for the night in record time as they were both exhausted. I than grabbed me a beer and plopped my butt on the couch to enjoy about an hour of "me" time before I passed out. Today was busy, hot, and fun. I enjoy my children very much, but I also enjoy my wife very much too. One day down, two to go. I can make it, I know I can make it, I have to make it. When I do make it alive I will crack open a bottle of champagne and celebrate my victory.

Wednesday

Today the girls and I, along with a couple of mothers from our weekly playgroup and their children, decided to venture out to the new mall that just opened up over the weekend. I am not one for shopping malls, but I was totally up for this as it was a way to get out of the house and share adult contact. I am glad we went as McKenzie got to pal around with other kids her age, and I was able to engage in conversation with people my age as it wasted about four hours of the day. We came home just in time for their afternoon naps as the day was flying by. After their naps, we ate a fast dinner and went to one of my "happy places," a brand new home improvement store. I didn't have to worry about the wife nagging at me. I was able to browse as long as I wanted to. The girls were very content as McKenzie likes going to these types of stores as much as I do. She loves all the tools and machines as much

139

as her Daddy. We spent about an hour and a half looking around before the girls finally ran out of patience and it was time to go. I could never spend and hour and a half there with my wife as she gets bored easily and demands to leave as soon as I walk in the door. Today was another busy day as the girls fell asleep swiftly and gently, as I grabbed a beer and plopped my butt once again on the couch to enjoy some "me" time. Two days down, two to go. Friday cannot come soon enough. My patience has been pretty good, but I have bad feeling the next couple of days are really going to test them. I am half way done with my mission, but I also have a long way to go. I can't look back, I must look forward. I am keeping to my battle plan as well as General MacArthur did and there is a light at the end of the tunnel, but I hope it is not a train!

Thursday

Day number three of flying solo as tomorrow my lovely wife will be back from her business trip and I will play quarterback and hand off the girls as soon as she walks in the door. My patience is surprisingly holding up as it is actually getting easier by the day as I am now used to not having any relief come nighttime. Today I am traveling over to the west part of town to spend time with my friend's wife and her two kids. They have a boy a few months older than McKenzie, and a baby a few months younger than Josie. My friend and I are very much alike. We were roommates in college for four years and together we really never had any problems with each other what so ever. His wife on the other hand is unlike me, she is the complete opposite. I spit, she swallows. I like her, we have no problems with each other, but I have never spent any time with just her without my friend being there. I was a little nervous that our personalities would clash, but I knew sooner or later I would have to find out if we would be able to be in the same room alone together without hating each other. The day went on without a hitch. We arrived at their house early in the morning. The kids played for awhile in the house then we decided we needed to do a little shopping as I needed to buy a birthday gift for a little boy in our playgroup that is having a party on Sunday. We picked up lunch on the way back as we all ate together like one big happy family. After we ate I took McKenzie and their son to the pool while my friend's wife stayed back with the two babies as they took a nap. We stayed at the pool about an hour as it was late in the day and it was time for us to go. I hugged my friends wife on the way out as I couldn't believe how well we got along. We both realize in each other's mind that we are very different, but we both have something in common, we love our children very much and will do anything for them. The more we spend alone together the better it will get. I have no problem hanging out with her as I hope she has no problem hanging out with me. Since the day was spent away from our house, the girls were very tired because they didn't get to nap at their usually times. The night came very fast as both girls went to bed early as Daddy was happy about that. One more day I kept repeating in my mind to help me through the day. After I laid my girls to sleep with a kiss on their foreheads, I celebrated end of the day with a chocolate chip ice cream cone and a ball game on television. Life is good, but life will be better when Lisa walks through the front door and says, "Honey, I'm home."

Friday

I woke up this morning with a smile on my face; today was the day my beloved wife and the mother of my children would be home. She told me last night on the phone that she should be home around dinnertime; I planned out the day as any other normal Friday. At 2 pm Lisa called and stated she was still there and didn't know what time they would be leaving, but reassured me that they must leave today since they have no hotel rooms reserved for the night. All day long I have been telling McKenzie that Mommy would be home today and she was really excited. I didn't want to break her heart, but I would have to. At 4:30 pm Lisa called again and stated they are still working and would keep me updated on when she would be coming home. I didn't worry, I just figured she would be home late in the evening. After dinner I took the girls to the pool to cheer up McKenzie as she was very sad her Mommy wasn't home yet. We stayed at the pool a long time and for the first time Josie didn't mind being in the water. When I walked in our house, I saw the red button flashing on the phone meaning there was a message waiting for me. I assumed it was from Lisa letting me know the time they had left and when to expect her home. That was not the case. She did leave a message, but the message was that she was not coming home tonight and basically had no idea when. I was calm and patient all week, but all my anxiety came to boil all at once as soon as I finished hearing her message. I thought for a moment she was kidding, but I knew she wouldn't do that with the girls emotions involved. I couldn't believe she wasn't coming home tonight as I had the tearful duty of telling McKenzie her Mommy would not be home to tuck her in her bed as I have promised to her all day. Not only do I have to break her heart, what about my golf game I have scheduled with my friend in the morning? He and I have been looking forward to the golf game all week, now I can't go. What the hell am I going to do? My mind started racing as I had no way of getting a hold of Lisa, I just walked around in circles what seemed like hours not knowing what to do or say. I calmed down enough to put Josie to bed, as I broke the bad news to McKenzie. She didn't take it well as there were tears in her eyes. I gave her what ever she wanted to eat as I put on a video for her to watch. That is when I got busy with my plans. I was going golfing tomorrow hell or high water. Just as I was thinking of how I was going to manage going golfing with two kids, Lisa called. Things really got screwed up at work as she promised me no matter what else might happen, she will be home at 11am in the morning even if she had to rent the concord to get home. That was all the information I needed to get a plan into action. I needed to leave my house at 6:30am in the morning to make my scheduled tee time. I first called our babysitter and she said she could be at our house at 9 am in the morning, step one complete. I then went across the street to our neighbor who has been telling me since I have moved in she will watch the girls anytime I needed. Well I needed her as I begged her to come over at 6:30am until 9 am in the morning as I explained to her the situation I am in and the plan to get me out. She had no problem coming over as she was thrilled to watch my girls. I then got on the phone and called two other neighbors as I explained the situation and asked them if they could stop by in the morning to make sure everything is going ok with the babysitter and to keep an eye on my babies until Lisa got home. They both agreed they would come by. My plan is totally in motion, as I now have to explain what is going to happen in the morning to McKenzie. I began feeling guilty leaving my babies alone with a neighbor as I selfishly go to play golf, but I need to get out bad. I figured the girls wouldn't get up until 8 am, leaving our neighbor to watch them for an hour. Our babysitter would get there at 9 am, and watch them for two hours as Lisa would get home by 11 am. Everything seems to be in order as I prepare notes and breakfast before I went to bed. I tossed and turned all night worrying how Josie will react when I am not there in the morning, but I made my bed, I now must lie in it. Lisa was to call my cell phone number in the morning to let me know exactly when she was leaving. I also left the number for the sitter in case of any problems. I was covered from head to toe on the operation. I explained what was going to happen in the morning to McKenzie and she seemed to be excited about it as I told her she must be the "Mommy" and take care of Josie until Mommy came home. I wasn't worried at all about McKenzie as I know she would be able to tell our neighbor and babysitter exactly what to do, I was really worried about Josie. How is Josie going to react when she wakes up in the morning and a stranger is there to pick her up? Our neighbor is no stranger, both the girls waive to her so they know who she is, but she has never watched them before. That is the part of the plan that made it very nerve racking. I put all my worries aside as my plan should go off without a hitch as I made sure of every last detail. It took me awhile to fall asleep as the guilt and the worry began to eat me alive, but something in the back of my mind kept telling me not to worry about it and go golfing, so I did.

Saturday- the execution of the plan

6 am Woke up, got dressed prepared for departure.

630 am Our neighbor arrived as I went over everything with her about the girls' morning routine.

7:15 am I received the call from Lisa letting me know she is on her way home.

7:20 am My friend and I teed off on the first hole. I parred the hole.

8:30 am I made my first call home to check on the girls. McKenzie answered and sounded good as she was having a good time. I talked with our neighbor and she was having a great time watching the girls. Josie was perfect.

10 am I made a second call home to check on the babysitter. McKenzie answered the phone again and called me a pest. The babysitter states everything is perfect.

11 am. Lisa calls, she is home. A smile breaks out in my face.

11:45 am We finish our round of golf.

11:50 am I drink a cold beer to celebrate my victory and my master plan.

12 pm I begin my drive home as I look forward to seeing all of my girls.

1 pm I walk in the door and life if back the way it should always be, all together as one happy family.

Week 47
August 23rd-27th

Tuesday

Life is finally back to normal after last week's endurance test. Today was our weekly playgroup in which I had to sacrifice my own child for the good of the playgroup. With September a week away, many of the children in the playgroup will be attending preschool, McKenzie being one of them. We had to decide as a group which day would be best for all involved to continue meeting on a weekly basis. I hate to stereotype, but me being the only man in the group; I had to take charge because as usual, the women couldn't make up their minds. What I did was write down all the days each of the different children would be in school, then by elimination I figured out which day would fit best. As I began sorting out the best day, my heart began to thump a little faster as it appears that Friday would fit best for everyone, everyone that is except my little McKenzie. Friday was the only day all the children would be able to attend, except for McKenzie. I didn't reveal my little secret right away as I tried like hell to come up with a different day than Friday, but I couldn't. I then announced my decision to the group as they agreed that Friday would be the best day. I felt bad for McKenzie, but at least Josie will still be able to participate. I broke the bad new to Lisa and she wasn't very happy. I had to explain to her why McKenzie will no longer be able to attend, but she was still very upset. So being the great father I am, I told Lisa since McKenzie wasn't able to attend playgroup anymore, we can sign her up for another session of gymnastics. That perked Lisa right up as we discussed this with McKenzie and she was very happy to be going back to gymnastics class. McKenzie really enjoyed her first stint with gymnastics so she was happy to be going back for more classes. I skated on thin ice there for awhile with Lisa as I had to boot out my own daughter out from the playgroup, but rebounded real fast with the suggestion since she can't go to playgroup, she can go to gymnastics. In hockey, that would be considered a "great save." Lisa and I also discussed as McKenzie and Josie grow older, there will be many things that they will not be able to do because of other engagements. Lisa and I both agree that the playgroup is a great way to interact with the kids in the neighborhood, but school, sports and other outside activities will fill up our days faster than a squirrel's mouth full of nuts right before winter.

Thursday

Break out the champagne as Lisa and I have something to celebrate. There will be two new additions to our family; that's right twins! We are expecting two boys to be born anytime now as there names will be Tommy and Timmy. How do we know this? McKenzie told us as she states she has two baby boys in her tummy and will need to go to the hospital in a couple of days to deliver them. I don't know how she got the idea that she is pregnant, but it is quite cute. At first I didn't know how to react because even the thought of my baby being pregnant gave me an uneasy feeling in my stomach. Not because she is three years old, but I know there will come a time in her life when she is married that she will indeed be pregnant and I will officially become ancient in age as I will become a grandpa. If she has her babies now, I will become one of the youngest grandpa's in the world at the age of 32. That's nothing to joke about as I am sure there are plenty in the world who have become grandparents at such an early age. McKenzie is acting so cute though with the pretending of her pregnancy. She states she is having "two sons" and their names are "Tommy and Timmy." She keeps telling us that they are in "her belly" and their "heads" are always poking her from inside. The amazing thing is she tells Lisa and I with a straight face like she is dead serious. Her imagination is very good as people always say that girls imaginations are far better than boys. Even though McKenzie is only the ripe age of three, I know already in my heart when she does become a mother (hopefully twenty or thirty years down the road) she will be an extraordinary mother. She already is a very caring, loving and unselfish person, in which you need to be all of these when you become a parent. Just for curiosity sakes, we did ask her, "How her babies got into her stomach?" She replied that, "God put them in there," as we both looked at each other in amazement. We just started telling her about God and heaven as I am trying to explain to her that her grandma (my mother) will soon be going to heaven to be with god as she is very sick. She is very curious about heaven, as she asks all the time, "Who lives in heaven?" When she starts her preschool in a couple of weeks, she will learn more about God as part of her teaching will be the Bible. I am sure Lisa and I are going to have to answer a lot more questions as she learns and becomes more curious about the things she is taught at school. I just hope I am able to answer her as best I can. Until then, I will get the nursery ready for McKenzie's twins and make sure McKenzie is well rested for she is the one that will be getting up the middle of the night when the babies are crying wanting to be fed.

Tuesday

When you have children, some of the simple things in life you take for granted become some of the most difficult things to do. One of those things is having a simple conversation with your spouse. It is almost impossible for Lisa and I to hold a conversation, or even speak a sentence to each other without any interruptions from either Josie or McKenzie. Being interrupted once in awhile is fine, but all the time becomes very annoying. No matter how many times we correct McKenzie about not speaking when Mommy and Daddy are talking, she still continues to do it. It would be different if she had something important to say, but mainly she has nothing but child babble as I get frustrated real fast as I always have to stop in mid sentence to answer her. If it's not McKenzie interrupting us, Josie is there to take her place. Either by screaming for attention or grabs on to one of us to pick her up. It literally will take us 5 minutes to finish one sentence because of all the interruptions. By the time we are done with what we are trying to tell one another, neither of us can remember what was said. Our minds become so boggled we can't make sense of what we just heard. In fact, I have come to the point that I tell Lisa don't even talk to me until the kids are in bed so I can actually listen to her without any pauses or interruptions. The problem is even worse when we are driving. "What's that?" or, "Who's that"?" or, "What accident?" blah, blah, blah, that is all I here out of McKenzie's mouth. She is such a woman. Her mouth is always going with nothing of any importance coming out of it. She will talk just to hear herself. I have become very good at just tuning her out. I have to just so I am able to concentrate on the road. I have become so good at tuning out my girls, sometimes Lisa talks to me I don't even here her. That really drives Lisa mad, but I think my brain is programed to tune people out automatically when I need a rest. I knew going in, when we were thinking of having children that I would lose sleep and never have any money. I never expected that I would have to wait til nighttime for me to be able to hold a conversation with my wife. Maybe that is why couples who are having trouble with their marriages have children to save their marriage. If you can't talk to your spouse all day, you never get into arguments. When you are able to talk, it is late at night and everyone is tired. The only thing to do is sleep or have sex. Either choice is a good one so there can't be too many arguments brought up over sex and sleep. Lisa and I can go a whole day without speaking to one another and not affect our marriage. When the kids are up, we can't hold a conversation because of all the interruptions. We don't speak when we are asleep, and during sex there are short precise phrases spoke to one another that I do not believe constitute as an actual conversation. So whoever suggested having children can save a marriage might be right. You can't argue with one another if you are asleep, having sex or trying to answer questions like, "Why is the sky blue?"

Wednesday

One of the girls' favorite toys is this little girl figurine that can't be more than 2 inches big. McKenzie has named her Cathy. I call her the "Amazing Cathy" for many reasons. With so many toys, books, and other stuff the girls have in this house, many things often get lost and never found, but not Cathy. A few months ago McKenzie brought Cathy into a store when we went shopping. As I was loading up the car, McKenzie started to cry because she had lost Cathy. I didn't care, but McKenzie was very upset, so I headed back into the store to look around real fast knowing I would never find her to let McKenzie know I tried to find her, but couldn't. I couldn't believe it, but the second aisle that I happen to go down, Cathy was just sitting there among some other toys. As a miracle would have it, Cathy was found among thousands of other items within the store. McKenzie was very happy as I was just amazed that I was able to find her. When we went home over the Fourth of July, Cathy of course went with us. After about a week being at home after our trip, McKenzie once again was upset as Cathy was nowhere to be found. I thought for sure this was finally the end of Cathy as we would be able to move on with our lives. I mentioned to Lisa the last time I saw Cathy was at her brother's house lying on the floor next to the couch. Sure enough, Lisa made a call to her brother and Cathy was still on the floor next to the couch as last seen. Lisa's brother mailed her back to us the next day and Cathy is once again safe and sound back in our lives. Since then, Cathy has been lost then found over and over again. I can explain how she gets lost, but I can't explain it how she is found. There is something special about that little figurine that I haven't figured out. Is she McKenzie's guardian angel? I don't know, but it is really beginning to freak me out how this little 2 inch doll always seems to get lost, and when all hope is gone in finding her, she miraculously reappears. There is something about Cathy that just isn't normal. One day I am sure I will wake up in the middle of the night and open my eyes to see her staring at me. That is when I will take that doll and bury it in the ground, and then bury the shovel never to see that doll again. At least

I would hope I would never see that doll again.

Friday

For the last couple of months, I have been realizing that I am starting to lose touch of the outside world. I used to be very up to date on current affairs and what is happening locally and nationally, but lately I haven't a clue. I never have been interested in watching the news on television. I'd rather read the newspaper for information. With the paper I am able to inform myself on what I want to be informed on instead of listening to a news channel and having to sit through many unworthy news stories to listen to the ones I am interested in. It is easier to sort through a paper and read the articles I am interested in. I also believe a newspaper is much more thorough than a television newscast. As of late, I haven't been able to read the newspaper on a daily basis. I would never go a day without reading the paper when I worked, but now it is becoming more and more difficult for me to find time to read the paper or have enough energy to do so when I am able. I am getting more and more out of touch with the real world and that is beginning to scare me. I remember talking to one of my friends' wives back home who is a "stay home mom." I couldn't believe it when she told me she couldn't even turn on a computer if she had to. I couldn't believe that someone actually could become so tuned out of other things in life when you stay home to raise a family. I just thought maybe she was dumb or lazy, but now I know why she can't turn on a computer, she is busy raising children. Even when I might have the time to do other things when at home, reading the newspaper usually doesn't rate high on the priority list. Naps, housework and watching a little television usually rates high on the priority list. I do however always find the time to read my weekly sports magazine. I am still a man and I am dedicated to know as much as possible about all sports. When I become ignorant about sports somebody better check my pulse because I might as well be dead. I am really going to be a busy beaver starting next week when McKenzie starts going to pre-school three days a week. I will be able to spend a lot more time with Josie on a one on one basis without the bothersome McKenzie. I am really looking forward to that. As my girls grow, so will my daily chores. I don't know when I am going to have time to read the paper or watch television as my days will most likely be filled with chauffeuring my girls around from one activity to another. Will I become a dullard? Will I become one of those people that didn't even know the Berlin Wall came down? I don't know but I am heading that way. Being a "stay home parent" takes total concentration dealing with your children so the outside world takes a back seat to one's reality. I am lucky enough to know what day of the week it is or even the date of the month most of time. If I get that right I am happy. I can't explain it but it is like traveling into a black hole. I might not know what the Dow Jones closed at for the week, but I do know that macaroni and cheese was on sale at the grocery store.

Week 49
September 6th-10th

Wednesday

I woke up this morning with one of those big smiles on my face just like the ones I saw on other parents faces a couple of weeks ago. Today is the first day of school for McKenzie. I am happy for myself and for her as I believe she was getting bored at home during the day and needed more stimulation. It is no fault of McKenzie's that she is bored, more fault goes to Lisa and I. McKenzie has mastered all her puzzles, she is sick and tired of her books as she has heard them over and over too many times, and the computer programs don't challenge her anymore. Lisa and I cannot keep up with her intelligence as every time we buy her something new, within a week she is bored with it. This is why we have decided to send her to pre-school three times a week for four hours a day. She will be in school, Mondays, Wednesdays and Fridays from 9:30 am-1:30 pm. I don't even get to eat lunch with her anymore on those days as she is really beginning to grow up way too fast. It took no convincing that four hours a day, three times a week would not be too much for our little 3-year-old girl. McKenzie is so interested in learning, and being with kids her own age, she could probably handle going 5 days a week, 8 hours a day. I am not ready to let my baby go for that long as I am excited for her and also a little sad to see my baby gone from my arms that amount of time. I am looking forward to the time that I am going to be able to spend with Josie one on one while McKenzie is in school. Some of my first tasks with Josie is getting her to talk, use silverware, and the dirtiest task of all, potty training. Josie is behind the progress compared to her sister. It is now my job to buckle down on Josie and get her up to speed, so when it is time for Josie to go to school, McKenzie's old teachers won't ask Josie, "Why can't you be as smart as your sister, McKenzie?" I do think about the future when they do go to school together as McKenzie will set the standard and Josie will have to meet it. I can see it now when McKenzie comes home with straight A's and Josie does not, McKenzie will of course call Josie a "dummy." Then Josie will calmly walk over to McKenzie and punch her in the nose. There will be a lot of crying and fighting as these two grow up, but I have a front row seat to see it all. As Lisa and I walked McKenzie into her classroom, my little girl was both nervous and excited. We let her begin playing with the other children to make sure she was comfortable before we snuck out. Lisa didn't cry as I expected her to, but she was very proud of her daughter. As I waited in the car pool line to pick her up after school my stomach began to tie into a knot. Thoughts raced through my head like "Did she like school?" "Did she make any friends?" "Does she like her teacher?" I didn't receive a phone call to pick her up so I guess everything went ok. As I was approaching my turn in line I could see her blond hair beginning to makes its way out the door. As I pulled up she walked out with the biggest smile on her face as if she just won the lottery. I picked her up and gave her a big hug as I placed her inside the van. I asked her, "How was school?" She replied, "I love school Daddy, when can I go back?" I was very happy to hear her response, but also a little sad. I am very happy she likes school and wants to go back, but I am also sad at the same time as she is beginning a life without her Daddy taking care of her. She talked about school all the way home as I just listened to the joy in her voice. My baby is growing up, growing up real fast as I look next to her and see her sister sitting there growing just as fast. When you are a child all you want to do is grow and be big. When you are a parent, you want your children to stay babies. Today was a reality check for me that my babies aren't babies anymore, it may be time to make a third. Maybe that is.

Friday

I have a little more free time on my hands now that McKenzie is in preschool three times a week. Today as Josie was taking a nap; I sat on the couch and thought to myself how much easier it is to take care of one child, rather than two. It also gave me a lot of time to think what I really do all day as I stay home and raise my two daughters. Mostly it is the same thing over and over and over again. Let me give some examples:

Open and close our refrigerator, 102 times a day
Open and close our pantry, 72 times a day
Change Josie's diaper, 5 times a day
Pick up the girls toys, 23 times a day
Answer our telephone, 15 times a day
Wash our dishes, 3 times a day
Say the word "no", 2,205 times a day
Answer "because" after the question of "Why?" is asked, 1,025 times a day
Yell at our dog to quit barking, 75 times a day
Walk up and down the stairs, too tired to count

151

The number of times I smile as I see my daughters growing up in front of my eyes, infinity

Put all of the above list together and it is a typical day for me. Some of the numbers may have been exaggerated a little. I however am certain of the number of times I say to myself, "I would rather be at work right now than staying home raising my daughters." That number is zero.

Monday

   Ever since I became a father, I have always tried to keep things in perspective, especially with McKenzie. Lisa has always praised her from day one as being "special." Every parent around the world wants to believe at least one of their children as being "The golden child." I have even nicknamed McKenzie the "golden child" on occasions when Lisa comments on her abilities. I have downplayed some of McKenzie's abilities because I don't want to be one of those parents who think their child is the greatest thing since sliced bread. As I have been home with McKenzie now for 49 weeks, I am beginning to understand why Lisa believes McKenzie is "special." It is hard for me to admit that McKenzie might actually be the greatest thing that this country has seen since sliced bread. I am starting to admit this because of all the comments other parents make regarding McKenzie. The only way you can judge your children's abilities is from other children in the same age bracket. When people see McKenzie for the first time they often mistake her for a four-year-old because of the way she handles herself. I won't get caught up in the fact that she might be smart for her age or even advanced. I just don't know what advanced really means. I don't care what advanced really means because I want her just to be as normal a 3-year-old girl should be. I guess we will find out in a few years when McKenzie starts going to school if she really is advanced among children her age. I believe children in this day and age have the ability to grow up smarter and to be more intelligent than when I was growing up. There are more educational programs on television for children to learn from. At age 3 McKenzie has already mastered the computer. I didn't touch a computer until I was 16 years old. Most schools if not all have computers for children to learn. With the internet, information is basically at children's fingertips, unlike when I was growing up the library was my source of information sorting through countless books. Various educational only toy stores are becoming more popular as they are making educational toys as fun as regular toys. With all of this, children should grow up smarter and more ready for the real world much better than when I did. Then again, no matter how much is out there, a child still must have a good upbringing that starts from the home. It all begins and ends with the mother and father raising a good sensible child and not a child raised in day cares by society. Since my wife believes McKenzie is so smart and is going to grow up to be the next Einstein, we somehow have to come up with thousands of dollars a year to send her to private schools. My wife insists that the public schools in our area just aren't good enough. No matter what the cost is we will send her to them, even if I have to give up my golf. Yes, that is right, I will give up my golf if need be to send my daughter to the best schools to shape her mind. That is the kind of father I am. Will I be happy, maybe not, but Lisa will be and the old saying goes if Mommy is happy, everyone is happy. Time will tell if Lisa and other people are right about my McKenzie. Will she discover a cure for cancer? Will she be the first female president of the United States? I don't know. She might just get married and have children and raise them the best she can. No matter what she decides to do, if she is half as happy as I am, she will be one of the happiest people on the planet.

Tuesday

"God giveth, God taketh away." That's how I feel sometimes as I look at my two daughters. One daughter is as perfect as an angel, an almost perfect human being. Then there is Josie. Josie would make the most potent man in the world go get a vasectomy. She is trouble with a capital "t." I love her to death, she is my little "Snuckers", but sometimes I look at her and I can't believe that she is growing up in the same house, being raised by the same parents, as McKenzie. She is the complete opposite of her sister. McKenzie has long hair, Josie's has short hair. McKenzie is very interested in learning, Josie is very uninterested. McKenzie listens very well, Josie listens as well as a deaf person. McKenzie likes to read books, Josie like to rip books apart. There are many other differences between the two, but I love them very much the same. Actually, I am happy that I don't have carbon copies of children as each has it's own identity and personality. Josie is a lot of fun as she will purposely not listen to you and run away laughing as you chase her. She is more energetic and mischievous than McKenzie ever was at 18 months. I am guessing she is just your typical 18 month old causing parents havoc. Josie is always laughing and smiling as she knows she is causing trouble as she looks at you waiting for Lisa or I to react towards her. Josie is a problem child that I love having. McKenzie is so predicable and sincere I know exactly what to expect out of her on any given day, unlike Josie each day is a new adventure. Will Josie be in a good mood, or a bad mood? What will she break today or will I be visiting the emergency room? In our old house when McKenzie started to become mobile, I went out a bought cabinet locks and installed them on all our cabinets. She never once even tried to open a cabinet. I decided not to put on the child locks in this house as I figured if McKenzie wasn't into them, why would Josie. I am so wrong on that assumption as every two minutes Josie is inside a cabinet whipping whatever is inside them onto the floor. As I yell at her to stop, she does her usual, looks as me, laughs and runs away. Having Josie really keeps me on my toes, as I cannot sit down. I have lost weight while being at home with her. I cannot sit down for longer than 5 minutes as I have to dart out of my chair to chase her down to get her to stop whatever destruction she is up to. It amazes me how siblings growing up in the same house can turn out so different. It is assuring that my girls will grow up with different paths and different interests. It is way too early to tell but I think McKenzie will become a doctor or a lawyer, as Josie will grow up to be a construction worker or a iron welder. They both adore each other as they will never have to worry about growing up alone, they will always have each other to depend on and lean on each other in times of need. All the expectations of greatness has fallen on McKenzie at an early age. My money is on Josie as she has no pressure on her as it is all on her sister. This way Josie can just do her own thing and surprise all of her critics. It would be ironic if Josie turns out to be the star as McKenzie lives with us until she is 45 years old and works at McDonald's. Actually, no it wouldn't!

Friday

A horrible tragedy occurred in our area involving a death of a 3-year-old boy. A father of another boy decided to give his 15 year old son his first driving lesson by letting him drive the family car into their driveway. Seemed harmless at the time. As the 15 year climbed into the drivers seat to drive the car into the driveway, a 3 year old and his 6 year old brother who live next door to the teenager, decided to watch harmlessly on the sidewalk. That is when everyone's life would change dramatically forever. As the 15 year put the car into drive, he pushed too hard onto the gas peddle as the car took off out of control and violently ran over the two boys who as they watched. The 3 year old died of massive chest injuries, and his 6 year old brother survived, but sustained serious injuries. Life will never be the same for the 15-year-old boy, the father of the boy, and the parents of the dead child. Life without warning can take such a cruel turn without any warning. How will the 15-year-old boy go on with life knowing what has happened? Yes it was a complete accident, but the outcome might be too devastating for him to even attempt to get behind the wheel of another automobile. What about the father of the boy who let his son take his first test at driving? The guilt and the shame he must be feeling being a father, knowing the pain the parents of that precious 3-year old boy must be going through. The parents of the 3 year old boy who thought the day was just another ordinary day, now have to bury one of their own flesh and blood at such an innocent age. Life will never be the same for any of the people involved. All of this mayhem from the simple act of driving a car 5 miles an hour into a driveway. God must work in mysterious ways and sometimes I don't understand it. Can something like this happen to one of my daughters? Everyone believes something horrible like this won't happen to them, but there are no guarantees in life and you never know what the future holds. There are many pros and cons having children. The biggest con is the worry parents endure once they bring a child into this world. Having to deal and cope with the death of a child has to be the worst nightmare for any parent. I know it is for me. My sister had to bury her 2-year-old son after a battle of heart disease. Losing a child to an illness doesn't lessen the pain in any way, but at least it couldn't have been avoided. Losing a child to cancer, or the way my sister lost her little boy, has to be a little more comforting to live with knowing the child's pain and suffering are over and they are in a more peaceful place. Having a child taken away from a parent by something that could have been avoided must rip the heart and soul out of you. Forever and ever those parents will be asking themselves "what if" for the rest of their lives. What if I was outside watching over my boys, this never would have happened? What if the father of the driver decided not to let his son drive the car up the driveway? Nothing like this never would have happened. It is too late for what if's. I couldn't imagine or want to imagine losing one of my daughters in any circumstance. That would be the day that I would die inside if something tragic like this ever happens to my family. The biggest effect fatherhood has put on me is worry. I worry constantly about my girls and will as long as I live. God: "Look down on my daughters and protect them from harm. Let them live a long a prosperous life. They are my life now and if you decide to take them away, take me instead as then I can be the one to watch over them from above. Dad."

Monday

I can't believe that 50 weeks have gone by since I have decided to stay home full time and raise my daughters. It has gone by so fast it seems like it has only been fifty minutes instead of fifty weeks. I have only 2 weeks remaining until I have been home now for one full year. A lot has happened in the past fifty weeks to my family and me. After nine years working for the only company my wife ever worked for, she decided it was time for a change and got a new job. Her job took us to a new state 600 miles away as we left behind all our family and friends that we love very much. My mother was diagnosed with colon cancer and was given 3-12 months to live. My mother doesn't have much time left on this planet as her days of being my beloved mother is close to death as the cancer will soon take her life. My daughters have grown up so much in the past 50 weeks, I can't believe my eyes when I look at them and call them mine. My love has grown stronger for my wife, as she goes to work full time to support us financially, as I know she would rather stay home with her daughters. The biggest change of all in the past fifty weeks has been me. I have grown to love and appreciate every single day I am alive and well and spending time with my daughters as they grow beneath my care into little angels. I have been given the opportunity that very few men get in this world. I have grown as a person that I didn't think I could become. I love being a father and an everyday child provider. The next two weeks will be very sentimental for me as once they are over; it will be exactly one year that I will have been home. I will never get that year back in life, but I will always have all the memories of a wonderful time being with my daughters. Life and time goes by very fast. I am lucky enough to be able to stop and watch it go by without missing it.

Tuesday

I have officially been accepted by the neighborhood as a "stay home parent." In the mail today, we received a post card with an invitation to a pampered chef kitchen show at our neighbor's house down the street. It is like a Tupperware party but instead of Tupperware it is full of neat kitchen gadgets and ideas. Lisa has gone to 3 or 4 of them since we have been married and has bought several items. As I read the postcard for the time and date of the party, I noticed the time was for 10:30 am. I immediately thought that Lisa will be unable to attend since she will be at work at that time. Our neighbor knows she works full time so why did she bother to send her an invitation? Was she just being courteous and didn't want Lisa to feel left out? Or did she want Lisa to order products without actually going to the party? I didn't know. Then I read the postcard a little more carefully and it wasn't addressed to Lisa, it was addressed to me! I just started laughing that I just got invited to my first domesticated function in our new neighborhood. It made me feel real good that I have been included and not left out just because I am a man. I could of easily been ignored and not invited and I would have thought nothing of it. Instead I am thrilled and very excited that I have been invited as the other "stay home parents" who are all women, accept me for being a man. I think it is real nice of the woman to have invited me knocking down the stereotype that only women would be interested in going to something like this. I do all the cooking in the house anyway, I don't even know why Lisa went to those other parties to begin with. She wouldn't know a toaster from a blender. Lisa going to a cooking party would be like me going to a board meeting on how to increase sales. It just wouldn't be right. I will attend the party as I am one, very excited about the possibilities of meeting other people since we are still very new to the area, and two, to let her know how happy and pleased that she included me even though I am a man. It is people like her that make it easier for me to accept my role as a "stay home dad." Times are changing as more and more men are staying home as the women support the household financially. The more I tell people about our situation at home the more people tell me how wonderful it sounds and how happy I seem. I am happy and it is wonderful, and with more people like our neighbor who accept the situation, the easier it is to do. To show my gratitude, I will buy stuff even though I probably won't need it.

Thursday

I have just booked an emergency flight home to spend sometime with my mom. I received a call from my father stating the home care nurses have given my mother only 2-3 weeks left to live. Another part of me has died. I cannot endure the feeling and pain my mother is going through right now as I look at my own children I pray that they will never have to go through what I am going through right now. My mother is 62 years old. Young to die in this day and age of advanced medicine, but at least I had her for 32 years. Some people grow up without a mother or a father or both, I have counted my blessings. I cannot imagine my little girls growing up without their Mommy as they adore her so much. I can only hope and pray that they have their Mommy for a very long time. It is going to be a sinking feeling in my heart these next couple of days as I sit down and talk to my mom knowing this will the last time I will be able to talk to her alive. In her heart, she will know the same. I will tell her how much I love her and how much of a great mom she was to me. I will also tell her how much of a great grandmother she is to my daughters. I do feel blessed that I am going to be able to tell her these things before she passes away. This experience has been good and bad as our family has had to live each day with her death for 10 months. My mom is at peace with herself as she well should be. She has always put us children first and foremost before herself. She is the most unselfish person I have ever known as I know she has a place up in heaven right next to the Lord himself. As the tears fall down my face I can only say these final words: mom, I love you very much. I will never forget you.

Monday

This is it! The final hurdle, the last piece of the puzzle, the final countdown to the most extraordinary year of my life. This will be the 52nd week of my tenure of being a "stay home dad." It will be one full year exactly after these next 5 days have gone by. I can't believe it has already been a year. So much has happened within the year, one would think it was actually two or three years that has gone by and not only one. I am very excited that my first anniversary is about to become reality. When I decided to stay home full time, there were doubts in my mind if I was able to handle the responsibility of raising a family. Would I go crazy after just a few weeks? Would my wife come home from work as I sit in the corner twiddling my lip? Would I shave my head and live at the airport? I just didn't know how I was going to react and adapt to be the primary care giver. My doubts didn't come from being a man, but because staying home is such a huge task for anyone, I was just praying I be up to that task. With my year anniversary being just around the corner, I can look into the mirror at myself and smile from ear to ear. I have the ability to stay home full time and many people don't. Granted, most of those people that say they couldn't stay home all day are men, but I know plenty of women who do not like to stay home all day with their children. I, on the other hand, wouldn't have it any other way. This past year has made me realize how much time I have wasted when I was working. I had to work to make a living, but it is just amazing the time that is wasted doing so. My wife is happier now than ever as are our children. This week I will be doing a lot of remembering of the past 51 weeks as I look in the future to the next 1,000 weeks. I am sad knowing that the year has past by so fast that the following years will probably past by even faster. Life does go by at an amazing speed and that is why I am living everyday to the fullest. I am living them with my daughters.

Tuesday

McKenzie and Josie are really becoming two peas in a pod. It is monkey see, monkey do in the Major house. Having our daughters 23 months apart is starting to pay off dividends. It was hard having them so close in age, but we decided that if we were only going to have two children (the third child is still in debate, heavy debate) we wanted them back to back. If McKenzie has a snack, Josie must have a snack. If Josie has her milk, McKenzie must have her milk. One must not go without if the other has. It is amazing how intuitive they are to what the other is doing. They are beginning to play real nice with each other as they have the same interests. Josie still needs to learn how to play together because if she doesn't get her way the alien screech blurs out her mouth right into my eardrum. If she keeps this up for a long period of time, I will need hearing aids before I am 40. I cannot imagine having an only child. Seeing them playing together enjoying each other's company puts a huge smile on my face. They will not need to have any friends besides themselves, they are and will be forever "best friends." If we decided to have only one child, McKenzie wouldn't have a best friend at the age of 3 and a half, as I would be her only play mate. My days playing with dolls and puzzles ended a long time ago. I am now waiting for them to get older when they are ready to play with the easy bake ovens so they can bake me a cake that has been sitting in a box for two years. Yummy! McKenzie loves being the big sister as I believe Josie loves being the little sister. McKenzie is always looking out for her as Josie relies on McKenzie like she is her second mother. McKenzie helps her up and down the stairs, gets her milk, and lets me know immediately when Josie "stinks." If I can only get McKenzie to change her diaper my day would be a lot easier. McKenzie will become her second mother as Lisa and I will need her to be with all the trouble Josie is going to get into as she grows up. Next year the both of them will be going to the same school. That will be really weird as it is just the beginning of things to come. First school, then sports together, or cheerleading or dance. Whatever one is in, the other won't be far behind. As they grow up, my wallet will shrink. I am sure these two girls will put Lisa and I into the poor house. I believe it is time Lisa thinks about getting a second job. I will not be able to get a job as the girls will be used to me being there for them during the day, and at night I am too tired after being with the girls all day. I haven't broke the bad news to Lisa yet about the thought of her getting a second job. I saw in the paper that a sports equipment store is looking for nighttime stock personnel. That would be perfect. She would start at 10 pm and work until 7 am. She can then come home, take a quick shower, eat some breakfast and be at her real job by 8 am. Sounds like a good plan to me. Having children you have to learn to make sacrifices in life. I did by quitting my professional career to stay home and raise our daughters. Lisa will just have to work two jobs to support us. Sounds pretty fair to me, now I am going to have to convince Lisa of the fact. I don't think she will agree with my plan, actually I know she won't. It will be fun telling her as I am sure the look on her face will be worth the breath out of my mouth. I would never let her work two jobs to support us, as I would have to step up to the plate and get a job at night. The park district is looking for umpires to umpire little league games. That is the kind of work I want to do from now on. No more ties and suits. No more meetings and commuting. My jobs will consist of fun work such as umpiring or cutting grass at a golf course. I will call today to see if they still need umpires as it will be a good way to get out of the house at night and make some extra money. Once I get good at it and Lisa brings up having a third child again, I can raise my right arm and yell "you're out!"

Wednesday

Being that the weather is still delightful here in Atlanta, unlike Chicago where I am sure it is cold and rainy, many nights are still spent playing outside. Last night was no exception. After dinner we all went outside as a family to enjoy the weather as the girls played in front of the house. One of our neighbors came over with their 18 month old son. Josie enjoys it when he comes over as he is just about the same age as she is. One of the things McKenzie enjoys to do is to pull Josie in the wagon pretending she is the Mommy. She decided that she was going to pull them both, so she put our neighbor's son in the wagon along with Josie. Our wagon has a side door on it that enables them to get in and out. While McKenzie was shutting the door, she accidently shut the door on the little boy's finger. The door pinched his little finger as tears dripped down his face in agony. It had to hurt because I know when I pinch my finger in something, I want to cry. The boy made it through after a hug from his father, but McKenzie was the one affected most. She is a very sensitive little girl. After she heard him scream after she accidently shut the door on his finger, she immediately ran into the house very upset. I basically had to drag her out of the house as she than began to cry. It took a good 15 minutes to calm her down and let her know everything was alright with his finger and no one was mad or upset at her as we all know it was an accident. Lisa is concerned about her over sensitivity. She thinks when it is time for her to go to school that kids are going to make fun of her and she won't be able to stick up for herself because she is too sensitive. First of all, all kids make fun of other kids, it's part of the growing up process. No matter who you are, someone will make fun of you somehow. Kids sometimes can be some of the meanest and cruelest people on earth. I got teased all the time. I wasn't a big kid growing up so I got picked on by the bigger kids. I held my own though, mainly with my mouth. As they picked on me physically, I would usually come up with some insults regarding them and they would just leave me alone. If you stand up to bullies or kids teasing you, they would usually stop picking on you and move onto someone else. They don't like the conflict, as they are looking for an easy target and if you show resistance, they basically give up to look for easier prey. Even though I was small and an easy target, I never took any crap from anyone as I let my mouth and brains get me through the tough years of being a kid. I believe McKenzie will be the same way growing up as I was. She is very smart and very likeable. She will have many friends at school, which will help her shield herself from ridicule. The more friends a kid has, the less they get picked on. I had many friends around me all the time so I was not an easy target by any means. Bullies look for kids by themselves to pick on, as the bully is usually the biggest coward among the other children. McKenzie will never be by herself as she goes out of her way to make friends. Yes, McKenzie will get picked on by other kids, but everyone does. She will have to be able to handle it and not run away and cry. That is the worst thing she could do is let someone get to her and make her cry. I will have to teach her how to handle mean kids when they pick on her so she doesn't get labeled as an easy target. I am not worried at all about her sensitivity. McKenzie is 100 percent girl, but she can hold her own. I am very rough with her when we play as she holds her own ground. I give her pink bellies all the time, she never cries. I even put her in head-locks as we wrestle. It takes a lot of physical abuse from me to make her cry which proves to me she can hold her own when she wants to. Another reason I think she is tougher than Lisa thinks is over the summer when McKenzie and I were in the pool, I would throw her in the air as high as I could as she splash landed into the water. We would do this repeatedly even though sometimes she would get water in her eyes, nose and mouth. I threw a boy the same way I did McKenzie and he cried his eyes out. He was even 6 months older than McKenzie and I thought boys were supposed to be tougher than girls. This boy was a real baby as he said I threw him too high. He is the one that is going to be picked on in school, not McKenzie. I am not naive. I know there will be plenty of times when she might come home crying and upset from what some kids might say or do to her. I know with my help and knowledge on the situation, McKenzie will be able to deal with it for the next time it happens, she will be able to defend herself. I have been down that path and it is now my turn to teach my child how to out bully a bully.

Josie on the other hand will be that bully. I foresee many trips to school to visit the principal to discuss issues with my second daughter's behavior. Josie should be able to get away with things in the beginning since she will be following the legacy McKenzie is going to leave behind, thus giving Josie the benefit of doubt. Within time Josie's luck will run out as it will soon be discovered that Josie is nothing like her big sister as trouble is bound to be wherever little Josie is. I will have to handle and deal with both worlds, the good and the bad. It should be very interesting watching and loving them as the grow up. I just wish it wouldn't go by so fast as people always tell me to enjoy your children now as the grow up so fast. All those people are right, they do grow up fast, but I am watching and enjoying every minute of it.

Thursday

It is time once again for us to do the dirty deed. It is round two as Josie is now 18 months old and Lisa is begging me to start potty training her. I believe potty training is the hardest thing to go through in regards to child rearing. The late night feedings, the crying, the diaper changing, the bottle feeding, the teething, and so on all take a back seat to potty training in my mind. Lisa also agrees that potty training is the most stressful, hardest and time consuming task of them all. We started real early with McKenzie because Lisa was pregnant with Josie, we didn't want two children in diapers. Not only would the smell kill us, so would the expense of buying countless diapers. McKenzie was 14 months old when we started to potty train her. She was completely trained at 18 months. It was not easy as we spent countless hours in the bathroom with her waiting for her to go on the potty. Our nanny had to do the brunt of the dirty work. Lisa and I both worked, so that meant she had to make sure McKenzie went on the potty during the day, as Lisa and I only had morning and nighttime duties. At least back then, Lisa and I got a break from it during the day, not this time. I get to do it full time as Lisa still escapes the havoc of it during the day as she gets to go to work. I can be honest, I hate it. It is such a pain and it wastes so much time during the process. Don't get me wrong, it is only to my benefit to get Josie trained as the expense of diapers and baby wipes are reasons enough to train your child as soon as you think they are ready. I believe we have started our girls earlier than most parents would, but we believe the sooner the better. I heard in Russia all the children are potty trained at 1 year old. I don't know if that is true or not, but I would love to send Josie to Russia for a couple of weeks to get her trained. Josie has already peed and pooped on the potty as a result of our training. McKenzie would literally sit on the potty for a half-hour to an hour before doing anything. With Josie it has only taken a few minutes after putting her on the potty for her to go to the bathroom. The difference I believe that Josie will not be consistent in telling Lisa and I when she has to go potty like McKenzie did. Josie will continue going in her diaper when she is not sitting on the potty. Another obstacle is McKenzie was talking very well at 18 months compared to Josie. Josie will not be able to tell us when she needs to go unlike McKenzie who was able to do so. I am afraid, very afraid of the next few months. Josie is all about a good time, not about learning. She will make a game of this because she will think it is funny to poop in her pants as I am trying to get her to poop in the potty. It isn't because she isn't smart enough to get potty trained, she is smart, too smart for her own good. She will realize what we are trying to accomplish and she will do the opposite to get a laugh out of it. I foresee cleaning up various Josie brownies as she will leave for me on the floor, or in her pants, or in her crib, as soon we will just have to go diaper free to get our point across. I am afraid, very afraid. The girls will learn some new words from Daddy before this is all over, and they won't be pleasant by any means. I have always thought that Josie will be the one that puts me in the grave, I just didn't think it would be this soon.

This is it; tomorrow is my one-year anniversary of being a "stay home dad" I can't believe it has already been one-year as it seems to have been only one week. Tonight I will lay in bed thinking of the past year and what it has meant to my family and me. I guess I won't be sleeping tonight as there is plenty to think about and to remember as this past year is filled with wonderful memories.

Friday

I woke up this morning with a huge smile on my face, along with some slight tears in my eyes. Today is the day we celebrate the one year anniversary of me staying home full time to raise my daughters. The smile is for the joy and wonderment of the year past by. The last 52 weeks have been the most gratifying any one man can ever experience. The tears in my eyes are also for the past 52 weeks. My babies are now a year older as they continue to grow up so fast as I will never be able to get that time back that I have just endured. That is one of the many reasons why I decided to quit my profession to stay home with my girls. Time goes by way too fast. I can write forever about the past year, but I won't. Today I just want to hug my children as long as I can as a remembrance to myself and to my family, that staying home to care and raise our children is not a burden, it is a privilege. There are many dual working families for one reason or another. Some have to work to make ends meet; some work just to keep up with "the Jones'". Not me! I would eat worms if that is what it would take to be able to continue to stay home and raise my family. I will cherish today as I will spend every waking moment cradling my girls as they brought me more joy and happiness than any paycheck could ever bring me. There were many doubts and worries that Lisa and I discussed before we made our decision on me staying home. Those worries and doubts have long been forgotten as we couldn't be happier.

Staying home raising children is by far the hardest job in the world. It is the most underappreciated, under paid and underrated. I wouldn't trade my position with the anyone, as I am a "stay home dad" and loving every minute of it. I hear my daughters calling my name as they need me now. I must go and tell them that I love them as they tell me they "love me." That is all I need to survive is my kids telling me that "they love me." To quote the late and great Lou Gehrig; "Today, I feel like I am the luckiest man on the face of the earth!" I am.

Extra innings

To use the term of my favorite sport, baseball, my year of writing my experiences and thoughts may have concluded, but I still have much to say about my year of being a "stay home dad." Staying home this past year has opened my eyes to a whole new world. A world that can only be seen and experienced through someone who dedicates their every waking breath to the care of their children. I am no longer a rookie (another baseball term) as I have now been a stay home dad for 1 year. That qualifies me as a veteran. In a few years, after I have proven myself, I will be able to sign one of those huge contracts baseball players are now signing. If a baseball player is worth $100 million to play 162 baseball games a year, I am guessing a stay home parent is worth about $100 billion to be there 365 days a year for the rest of their lives. There is one thing wrong with that. I am not in it for the money (that's good because there isn't any). What staying home raising your kids is all about is the love and affection you are dedicating to your children by being there for them. I signed that huge contract when I brought my babies home from the hospital. There was no dollar amount or even a piece of paper. When our babies were handed to us the only contract there is, is love. Being a stay home parent is not for the weak, or the timid. It takes love, guts, patience, the will to survive, strength, responsibility and much more. It takes all of that just to make it through some days, let alone the rest of your children's lives. It is a beautiful day for a ball game, let's play two!

Baby manual

When you buy a new car, it comes with an owner's manual on how to operate all its functions. The same goes with a new VCR or a camera. A manual is included to help its owner learn to operate and use the device correctly. What do new parents get when they leave the hospital with their newborn child? A pat on the back, a few diapers, a blanket and a "good luck," along with a lot of smirks from the attending nurses and doctors. It is for sure that luck is exactly what you need when you begin raising a baby. You don't know what you're bringing home. It could be Rosemary's Baby or Damian for all you know. There are countless books published regarding child raising, childcare, and so forth. Are there books written exactly for your child? Your make and model? That answer would be "no." They are written by experts who take in all the research and development of babies throughout the world and try to prepare you for what situations that may occur those first few weeks as new parents. A baby can cry for numerous reasons. It may be hungry, or have a wet diaper. It may be tired, or sick. My favorite is the baby is just trying to drive you crazy. It really isn't but one comes to think so when all it has been doing for 12 straight hours is cry. It is then the job of the mother and father to find the solution to your child's reason for crying without the help of any owner's manual. When you want to set the correct time on your VCR, it can be found within the manual. How to change a tire on your car can be found within your car's manual. When your baby begins to cry, a sudden rush of adrenalin and panic begins as your brain works in overload to try to resolve the situation as quickly and calmly as possible. You don't have time to dust off and start reading the dozens of books you may have bought to help you with your baby. With your baby crying in the back ground, it is now code red. Your baby has just gone on attack mode. First you try to feed your baby. If that doesn't work you begin to rock the baby. Why is it when you rock a baby standing up they love it? But once you sit down and rock your baby, the crying begins as if you are not rocking them at all. Does your child know your back is on fire and thinks it is funny? Mine sure thought it was funny. I would rock them standing up, everything was peaceful. As soon as I sat down, whaaaaaaaaa as if I wasn't rocking them at all. If the rocking doesn't work, you might try stimulation with toys or annoying baby talk. No matter what you may try, there is no clear way of getting your baby to stop crying. Forget about reading books, or listening to what others may tell you, get to work on your baby and figure it out. Trial and error is the name of the game the first few weeks. If first you don't succeed, try and try again. If you don't know how to change the film in your camera, you simply look it up it the manual. Within a few minutes, your film is changed and you are now an expert. That doesn't work that way with a baby. It takes time and patience and a lot of frustration to finally figure out how to care for you baby as it grows and becomes comfortable with you, and you become comfortable with them. Don't forget your baby was all warm and cozy inside Mommy for nine months. Now it is outside in the cold and has to look and depend on people twenty times his or her size. That can be quite scary. There have been many times I wish I could have climbed back in inside my mom's belly for safety. Your baby and you grow and learn from each other together. A baby's manual would be a gift from heaven if it was precise to only your baby's needs and wants. God above must have a very good sense of humor as he gives us the gift of life, but also enjoys watching the struggles and the triumphs we as parents go through trying to figure how to make our babies stop crying. I am not trying to take away from all the wonderful books people have written regarding babies. My wife and I have read a few of them. Did they do us any good? Yes. Can you live by them? No. All I am trying to say is every baby is different, which makes every situation different, which makes every resolution different. The books help to recognize problems, and offers different solutions. They may work, and then again they may not. As your baby is coming out of the mother's birth canal, how wonderful it would be that along with the umbilical cord, an owner's manual would also be attached for your convenience. That would be cool.

Death

The opposite of birth, of course, is death. I had to endure two deaths within my immediate family and neither was something I ever want to go through again, but unfortunately I will have to. First I had to experience the death of the only person in the world who I could always count on loving me and forgiving me for whatever I might have done. Good or bad, clean or dirty, I would always know that I was still loved by one, my mother. She lost her battle with cancer two weeks after I last visited her. I knew and she knew it would be the last time we would smile and tell each other how much we loved each other. I was strong and she was stronger. Neither of us cried as we looked in each other eyes remembering the 32 years we had together as mother and son. She was at peace and in a strange way I was at peace with her dying. Her body was so fragile and deteriorated from the black disease of cancer it broke my heart seeing her in that state. She deserved a better fate, and I didn't deserve such a wonderful mother. I could live a thousand lives and never live up to the standards she lived up to as being a mother. She is the definition of what a mother should be.

I got a call from my sister stating mother has about 48 hours left to live. I hung up the phone, not knowing how to react, so I did what most men do when they receive bad news. I headed for the liquor cabinet and started drinking whiskey and 7-up. My wife wondered to herself why I was drinking on a Sunday afternoon, and then really thought it was odd that I was drinking whiskey and not beer. Then I told her why I was drinking and why I was drinking whiskey, not beer. She then poured my next drink for me no questions asked. About three hours later and a few drinks down, the phone rang again. I just answered it not thinking who it could be since I was in my own little world by now, but it was my sister again. Mom was gone. Not 48 hours later, but only 2 or 3 hours later, it was over. Ten months to almost the day I found out my mother had terminal cancer, she finally found peace. My sister was crying and I just hung up the phone. What can I say to her that she doesn't already know? I did not want to talk to my father, no way! What can be said to him? Yes, I lost my mother, but he just lost his wife. I couldn't imagine what he was going through as he has just lost the most important person ever to come into his life. She gave him love, friendship, companionship, loyalty and most important, me and my brother and sister. Now she is gone and it is our job to be with him in his time of need.

I hung up the phone and told my wife. She was very strong and supportive for me as she sat down in the chair across from me and began crying like a baby, just what I needed. I just sat there as a million memories raced through my head. I couldn't move or speak. I was paralyzed in a way I can't explain. As my wife cried I drank. Life has just taken a left turn and nothing will be the same again for my family and me.

I'm not going to get into the details of the wake and funeral. It was just nice to see so many people come and tell me how much my mom meant to them. My mom had a lot of friends and I can honestly say no enemies. I still haven't cried over my mother's death. I felt like I needed to cry but I couldn't get myself to do it. I kept telling myself I needed to be strong but I don't know why. Probably because my mom was always strong. The strongest even on the day she died. I wish I had an onion I could peel and chop to make me cry. My wife of course cried the whole time. I couldn't believe she never passed out of dehydration. She is such a baby. Then it happened. The day of the funeral as we stood over her coffin for one last goodbye with just my brother and sister and my father. I was first to stand over her as my whole body suddenly turned into jell-O and my eyes filled with tears as I collapsed onto my mother's body as I hugged her as tight as my tired body would allow me to. I didn't want to let go. I just laid there with her as tears rolled down my checks as the words, "I love you Mommy," mumbled out of my mouth. I knew I had to let her go, but I couldn't. The onion has been peeled and chopped. I couldn't stop crying. I finally was able to let go with the help of my family as I walked out of the room. I don't know who I passed by or if I even talked to anyone. I just kept thinking to myself that I would never see my mom again.

How did my children react to their grandma dying? Just like most kids their age, they really didn't understand what exactly was going on. Josie was completely oblivious of the situation since she is way too young to understand, and I am thankful for that. McKenzie on the other hand kept asking over and over when grandma was going to wake up. That hurt me inside very much. It took a lot of tongue biting for me not to unleash tears whenever she would ask. Tears not for me, as I see my mother lying in her coffin, but tears for McKenzie, as all she wants is to be able to talk and be with her grandma like before. I can't make that happen. It's very strange as I am there grieving my mother's death as everybody comforts me, but I feel like I am letting down my daughter by not being able to wake her grandma up. She also wanted to know when she will see grandma again. I had to explain to her she will not see grandma again for a very long time. She wanted to know when? I had to explain to her that she won't see her again until she herself dies and goes to heaven. She wanted to know when that was going to be. As my nightmare wasn't big enough, I had to stress to her that it wouldn't be for a very, very, very, very, very long time. Did I mention I expressed a "very long time?" As McKenzie cried I assured her that grandma was in heaven looking down on her and will always protect her and take care of her. McKenzie goes to a preschool that has religion classes. She does understand there is a God in heaven and that is where people go when they die. She thinks it is cool how they become angels with wings. I think it is cool too as I know my mom probably has the biggest wings of any angel in heaven. McKenzie was very strong during the wake, almost too strong for a three and a half year old. I wasn't surprised, that is McKenzie. She is a strong, good-hearted little girl, and I would not expect anything less of her.

After only four months of losing my mother, I lost another member of our family; our beloved dog Brodie. Unlike with my mom in which I had the time to prepare for her demise, Brodie I did not. My wife and I always joked about how life would be so much more pleasant if Brodie wasn't around. Brodie really was a pain in the ass. I can't blame the dog, I can only blame Lisa and me. We got Brodie when she was only 6 weeks old. We just got married, just bought our first house and we weren't ready to have children yet so like many other blissfully happy newlyweds, we bought a dog. Brodie had the life for years until McKenzie was born. She was treated as if she actually came out of Lisa's womb. She ate my drywall, chewed on our end tables, ate my linoleum floor, bit me about 100 times and ran away at least 5 times. She was a bitch. Not just in definition, but a real live bitch. But she was our bitch and we loved her. Once the children came, Brodie knew her days of being queen of the castle were over. We tried everything in our power not to ignore her or treat her any differently, but our priorities changed and she became just a dog instead of our first baby. Brodie took offense to McKenzie and Josie as she pretty much hated them and hated us for bringing them into her castle. She wouldn't play with them and she often tried to bite them. As much of a pain in the ass as she was and did become, we still did love her.

Brodie did one thing very well and often, and that was eat. She would eat as much I would give her and wouldn't stop if there was food in front of her. I am guilty of giving her table food quite often. I figured that she is only going to live for 10 or 12 years, so I believed she should have a good 10 or 12 years and eat the food we did. Brodie did become overweight just a little, only about 20 pounds overweight! Then something very strange began happening. She began to eat less than normal and sometimes eat nothing at all. Her energy level was way down and Brodie just didn't seem like Brodie. She was no longer being the bitch I knew all so well. I decided to bring her to the veterinarian to see what could be bothering her. I was concerned as my emotions began to run through me as I was beginning to think something terrible was wrong with her. Unfortunately, I had to bring the dog to the veterinarian with my two daughters as they thought it was playtime with Brodie. They bothered her and bothered me, as they knew nothing of the situation. I had no tolerance wick that day as I often snapped my head off and yelled "just leave Brodie alone" about fifty times. To make a long story short (sorry, too late) the veterinarian took several tests, and explained to me that Brodie's kidneys are or have failed her. My heart dropped into my stomach as I looked into Brodie's eyes and she knew it was her time to go to the big dog house in the sky. She looked so sad and so tired. The doctor stated there are treatments we could try, but the test results were so severe, the outcome was forth coming, and that was death. I just went through this with my mother. Watching my mother slowly die a little each day I was not going to go through that emotional pain again with my damn dog. I know if my mother had to do it all over again she never would agree to all the chemotherapy she went though because her stage of cancer was so advanced there was nothing anyone or any treatment could do to save her. I felt the same way about Brodie at this time. Let the dog die with dignity.

My daughters kept asking me if Brodie was better now that the doctor has seen her. I just ignored them and wouldn't answer them honestly. They loved Brodie even though she wasn't very nice to them. Brodie did her best to dislike my daughters, but deep down she loved them too. Whenever we would wrestle or pretend fight on the floor, Brodie would go after me and protect McKenzie and Josie.

I got home and called my wife at her work. I told her Brodie's kidneys are no longer functioning and she must be put to sleep. I broke out in tears. My very sensitive wife on the other end of the phone began laughing as she thought I was making the whole thing up. Then she realized I wasn't joking as she recognized that tone in my voice that she heard just a few months ago.

We decided to give Brodie the best week of her remaining existence before we put her to sleep. McKenzie was absolutely crushed when we told her the news. I cried, again, Lisa cried and McKenzie cried. I cried for two reasons: I cried for the loss I was feeling for Brodie and the pain I am inflicting on my daughter once again. She just went through this ordeal of death with her grandma, and now she has to go through with it with her beloved house pet. It was one of the worst weeks of my existence as I knew by the end of the week, Brodie will no longer be biting me or my daughters, she will be gone.

Basically the whole week we held Brodie and told her how much she has meant to Lisa and I. Brodie wasn't really the girls' dog, it was mine and Lisa's dog. She was our first baby and it was a hard pill to swallow knowing Brodie will no longer be the pain in the ass we grew to love so much. As much as McKenzie was feeling sad, Lisa and I were totally devastated. Knowing Brodie was soon going to be gone, it was tearing us up inside more that we ever thought possible.

On Black Friday we took our last family picture with Brodie. The girls said their tearful goodbyes and Lisa and I just looked at each other as streams rolled down our own faces. We dropped the girls off at a neighbor's house as I didn't want them with us. As I said before, Brodie was our dog, not theirs, as we wanted to be with her ourselves just like the day we brought her home, by ourselves. We laid Brodie on the table as I never saw Brodie be more at peace. She knew what was going on as Lisa held her paw as the doctor injected her with the poison. She died almost immediately. When she died, a chapter in our life ended as we left the room holding each other shaking with grief.

We went for a drive and talked about Brodie the whole time. It was good to talk about her as we brought up the memories of when life was simple, a man, a woman and a dog. Life now is much more complicated than when Lisa and I started off as husband and wife. We went back to our neighbor's after a while and I picked up my daughters and gave them the biggest hug I ever gave them. My tears have dried as I am with my loving daughters who always bring happiness to me no matter what the circumstances may be. They are my ray of sunshine in a rainstorm. They are my reason I exist on this planet. If I ever had to go through what I just went through with my dog with one of them, I know this for a fact, that I would simply just die. To my sister that lost her first born son at the age of two, I am sorry. I couldn't and didn't feel her pain as I was only eighteen at the time and I thought the reason I existed was keg parties at college. But I was wrong, dead wrong. To anyone who had to endure the pain my sister went through, and still goes through, you have my deepest sympathy. It is my greatest fear in life, losing one of my daughters before it is my time to go. When I read stories of children dying in the paper, or listen to them on television, even though I do not know the people involved, my heart misses a beat as I sympathize for them. My whole perspective on life involving matters with children have completely turned around ever since I became a father. It is amazing the power children have over your soul. Rest in peace Brodie, we miss you.

Top 10 list

Every night, David Letterman reads a top 10 list on his talk show consisting of various topics. I have come up with my own top 10 list. My top 10 list contains the top 10 worries I have of being a parent of two daughters:

1. Kidnapping: absolutely my greatest fear as being a parent. Kidnapping is far worse than death. Kidnapping is always avoidable; death most times is not avoidable. Having a child kidnaped is like living a nightmare everyday of your life. There is no closure to the matter like there is with death. When someone dies, that is it. It is over and you must move on with you life. With kidnapping, it is never over. It is only over when you die. The reason it is never over is because there is no closure. Everyday for the rest of your life you wonder "where is my child?" "what is my child doing?" "Who took my child?" "Is my child still alive?" "Is my child suffering?" and "When is my child going to come home?" It is one of the most despicable crimes anyone can commit. People stealing other people's babies and children to sell them, to molest them, to try to make them their own, makes my stomach sick thinking about it. It is amazing to me that there are people out there that can commit such a horrendous act without even thinking about the lives they are going to destroy by doing so. Recently there was an episode about kidnapping on the x-files (one of my favorite shows of all time). The child was kidnaped while swinging on the swings in a neighborhood park. He kept calling for his

173

mother to push him, but she was too busy talking to another woman and sure enough, when she turned around to see why he stopped calling her name, he was gone. Just like that. After I watched the episode, the next few days while I was out in public with my kids, I had the tightest grasp on them wherever I went. I might as well have handcuffed them to my wrist because I was paranoid beyond belief. I am grateful of that episode as it reassured me of being a responsible parent and to keep all eyes on my children wherever I may be at all times.

2. Death: this one is pretty much self-explanatory. I pray everyday for the health and safety of my children. If cancer, or some sort of illness takes the life of one of my children I can blame God. God works in mysterious ways. In someway, somehow, would I be able to go on with life? An accidental death that could have been avoided, I could not go on living. Drunk drivers, or school shooting as example. I would have no mercy on the soul who takes the life of my daughters. God, please look after my daughters for a long and prosperous life. If you get lonely up there, take me instead.

3. Health: I have been blessed so far in life as being a very healthy person. Besides the common cold, I can honestly say I have never been terribly sick. I haven't even broke a bone in my body. I did however catch mononucleosis in college once that put me out of commission for about a month. I do remember how I received the disease, but I have to admit it was worth getting it. Runny noses, fevers, and coughs are an everyday occurrence when you have small children. I don't care about those things, I am more concerned about the big ones. I read and hear about other people's horror stories how someone's child appeared to be very healthy and normal, then the next thing you know, their child is dying from some dreadful disease. I worry all the time that something like that could happen to one of my daughters. I don't dwell on it and make my children live in a plastic bubble or anything. I cannot control what may happen or doesn't happen. All I can do is keep a careful eye out in watching their health.

4. Friends. Not the televison show, but true life friends. Friends for me has been as important as anything else in life has. My first true memories of anything has always been of all the friends I had growing up and how much they all meant to me. One of my favorite childhood memories has to be when I was about 5 or 6 years old. All the kids my age on my block had a big wheels. There had to be at least 10 of us who would just ride up and down the street all day long in our big wheels. It was the best feeling being surrounded by other kids, thus the start of lifetime friendships with all of them. I would

say at least once a week my big wheel would break from the constant use of it, but I had a neighbor who was a welder and he would always fix it. I am still very close to half of those big wheel buddies of mine, as I want my girls to have that too. You can never have enough friends in your life. A friend to me is as important as family members, sometimes more important. A friend is someone you can talk to about anything, especially when you can't talk to your mom or dad about something. A friend is someone you grow up with, sharing each other's good times and bad times. You make it through life together as a bond grows as you become close. To become someone's friend, you need to be unselfish, understanding, tolerant and trustworthy. These are all characteristics I would like my girls to have as they grow up to be adults. Building a friendship like anything, takes hard work and dedication. Anyone can say they have friends, but to say it and actually have friends are two different stories. I am now 600 miles away from all of my childhood friends. We still keep in touch and when I am in town and we get together, it is like I never left or haven't seen them in a while, that is true friendship. I would do anything for a friend, in which I have, that I wouldn't do for just anyone. In one instance I helped kidnap one of my friends. He was grounded by his parents for driving a car with out a license (big deal) and couldn't go with us to a rock concert. My other friends and I came up with a scheme to kidnap him so he could go with us to the concert. We were successful in doing so. The only punishment he received was when he came home he recognized his parents took off his bedroom door so he could no longer be able to plan anymore escapes in private. I think that was a pretty good price to pay for escaping as he was able to enjoy the concert. I want my girls to have the same experiences I have had with friends. I want my girls to have as many friends as possible. My mission has been accomplished so far. They have many school friends and neighborhood friends. A main reason my wife and I picked our subdivision was because of the overwhelming number of children in it. We could have bought a house in the country with more land, but with no people. I like living in a subdivision due to the fact there is someone always around that my children can play with. I know it is early, but my girls seem to realize how important it is to have friends and not just hang out with their Mommy and Daddy all the time. McKenzie is always asking if she can invite someone over to play with her. We always oblige as McKenzie is taking initiative to become someone's friend. I preach to McKenzie all the time how important friends are and how important my friends have been to me growing up. I also stress to her to treat a friend better than she would want to be treated. She understands as she has always been nice to her friends as they are always nice to her in return. It makes me feel good inside knowing that McKenzie realizes the importance of a good friendship. As soon as Josie gets a little older I will have to program her in the same way. I do know this though, they will always have at least one best friend in the world as long as they live. They will always have each other as their best friend.

5.Financial: raising kids is very expensive. I believe now that the average cost of raising a child from a newborn until they reach the age of 18 is $200,000 or more. Times that by two and I am in it for about a half of million. That is a lot of cabbage. Having two girls doesn't help the curve either. By the time my girls reach 18, I am sure our total is going to surpass 1.6 billion. My girls are expensive, but they are worth every penny. I can honestly say that I barely buy anything for myself. I finally threw away a pair of jeans that I had since college. Those jeans had to be over 14 years old. I buy my wife a lot of clothes though. I want her to look nice even though I don't. I want people to say, "How did such a good looking woman end up with such a slob?" I'm not that much of a slob, but my clothes are older than most fossils. It is worth the sacrifice of being able to give my girls whatever I believe it is important for them to have. I want them to be able to enjoy life to the fullest. Being on one income can be very stressful. Every penny counts, don't think it doesn't. There are times where we are lucky to make it through a pay period without bouncing any checks. It is worth the sacrifice being able to have a parent at home with them and not have my children stuck in day care. My wife and I are currently debating on private or public schooling for the girls. It is really McKenzie's fault we are having this debate. Every teacher she has had says she is "gifted" and far ahead of most of the children in her classes. I knew that the time McKenzie rolled off the couch and banged her head on the ground did some good, it knocked some sense into her. Lisa believes McKenzie will be bored at a public school and needs to be challenged, which private school will provide. Private school will cost us anywhere from five to ten thousand a year. We simply don't have it. I made a promise to Lisa that whatever it takes to send our girls to private school, if we choose to do so, I will do whatever it takes to make it happen. Working at night, weekends or simply donating my blood daily, I will do it. Lisa does not want me to have to work, but I see no other way of being able to afford private school without some sort of dual income. This is why sometimes I lay awake at night wondering how much more macaroni and cheese a person can eat. No matter how well you try to stretch the dollar, someone else is tugging harder on the other end of it. Raising a family on one income is very stressful and takes a lot of sacrifice and smart budgeting. Do we make enough to provide the girls with everything we want to give them? Most of the time I say no, but somehow we make it and I have the lumps of hair I find in the drain every morning to prove it.

6. School: as I mentioned before, my wife and are I are debating on what school we are going to send our daughters to. Will it be private school or public school? That is just the beginning of my worries when it comes to school. First of all, once my children begin going to school full time, I am going to be extremely lonely. I am already lonely the few hours they are both away together at school during the week. I am either going to have to have another child or even worse, get a job. Just saying the word "job" makes me cringe just thinking about it, but I will have to do something to keep my mind off my girls. I am also worried about their safety. School now a days seem to be the breeding ground for children that have serious issues for them to take it out on normal kids such as mine. School just isn't the safe haven you would like to think it should be for your children. I just hope when my girls go to school they are socially accepted by other kids. Kids are extremely mean and cruel if you are not accepted. I was always accepted because I did my own thing. I didn't care what other people thought, I did my own thing as my friends and I never had any problems. I know having girls their will be many issues to deal with such as cheerleading and clubs, and most of all boys. I want them to enjoy going to school as it really is more of a social activity than a learning institution. Parents think their kids are going to school to learn, they are not. They are going to school to socialize with all their friends. That's what school was for me, that and sports. I am not worried about them getting good grades because I know they will. McKenzie is very bright, Josie is average, but they have a mother who is very involved in their education and I know she will be on top of them to make sure their grades are what they should be. My grades were good enough to get into college, but more importantly I was accepted and school was never a problem for me. I hope my girls can work the system and be popular, but not too popular with the boys.

7. Dating: I have two beautiful, very attractive, blonde daughters. That means I need to invest in a double barreled shotgun before my daughters reach the dating age. One barrel for each daughter. I have already decided at what age my daughters will be allowed to start dating. That age will be fifty. That sounds about right to me. I hear it all the time when I am out in public with my daughters from strangers. "Wow, are your daughters beautiful." "You are going to have your hands full when they grow up." "The boys are going to be camping out on your front lawn to date your daughters." I just smile and say thanks, but what I really want to tell them is to "shut the____

up!" When my daughters turn fifty years old I will allow them to date. I believe then they should be mature enough to handle the responsibility. I will allow them to have a 10 pm curfew as I want to make sure they can handle the responsibility of dating before I let them stay out to 10:30 pm. As much as the thought of dating makes my stomach turn, I am going to make the best of it and totally torment my daughters and especially all the dimple faced little geek boys that come to my house to attempt to date my daughters. I was not afraid of Lisa's father when I came over to her house, I was terrified. There were times I wouldn't even go to the door because I could see her father nearby and I didn't want him to see me. I want it to be known when any unexpected victim of torture comes to my house they are entering "cape fear." Part of my responsibility as a father is protecting my children. A double barreled shotgun will be very good protection.

8. Marriage: this just makes sense. After either of my girls date about 50 or so losers, there will be one guy weeded out left standing in which he will have the privilege of marrying my daughters. He will not call me "dad", but "sir dad." I hope when either decides to get married, they marry the right guy. I have seen too many failed marriages with friends and family as pieces of two lives are left afterwards to be put back together like a puzzle. I can just hope and pray that when my daughters settle on a guy, he is just like me, perfect. It is going to be hard for me to keep my nose out of their love life, but I know I will have to let them make up their own mind no matter what I might have to say about the little creep. The candidates must do two things well, and do them very well in order to marry my daughters. They must first and always love them with all his heart. Second, no matter what the circumstance brings them in life, they must make them happy at all times. You don't have to be rich in life, just be rich in love, and love will always bring happiness. A sure fire way for anyone to gain the respect and love from me along with my blessing in their marriage to either of my daughters would be if he paid for the wedding and let me just sit back and enjoy the wedding day. I would then never have any problem calling him "son" or him calling me "dad."

9. The future of the world: will my children live and witness World War III? Are they going to live through another Great Depression? What other new diseases will they encounter? Will there be enough fuel, food, and shelter due to over population? These are very serious questions to very serious issues that face this world in the future. I lived through the Vietnam

178

War (but was only a baby to realize its impact) and the Gulf War. I have lived through a recession and the emergence of aids. It seems that every time I turn around someone else is dying of cancer. The world is a very cruel place, as you never know what is going to happen next. The only thing that is constant is change, and the world is definitely doing that everyday. My daughters are going to have to live and cope with many obstacles as this world is slowly becoming scarier to live in than a Halloween movie. What does the future hold? I don't know, but my daughters will experience it first hand and I have to admit it makes me scared for them.

       10. My daughters not needing their Daddy anymore: I want my daughters growing up to be self-sufficient. I don't want them to have to rely on anyone to get by, but I do want them always to want their Daddy. I read stories how children grow up and totally abandon their parents as if they don't even exist anymore. My heart would break if that happens to me. Don't get me wrong, I don't want them living in my house until they're forty, but when they move out and get married and have their own families, a call once in awhile telling me how much they love and miss me would make my day. I want to be involved in their life as much as possible without interfering. They will make mistakes and I hope they realize they can call on me to pick up the pieces and put them together again. I will make sure my daughters realize that I am their biggest fan and no matter where they are or what they do I will always love them and be there for them. I will not accept a phone call from them once a month asking me how I am doing. I must be needed and wanted even though I will become a wrinkled old prune. If the day comes where I don't feel needed or wanted, I will just have to move in with them to remind them I am still their Daddy.

Grandma finally arrives

      For months Lisa has been begging her mom to come visit us for a couple of weeks. She really has no excuse not to. She doesn't work, she lives alone, she lives in Chicago where the weather is cruel, and we would pay for everything. So what is stopping her? Herself and only herself. About 2 months ago Lisa got somewhat of a commitment from her mom over the phone to come visit and Lisa was all ready to buy her a plane ticket. The next day Lisa discussed it with me and asked me what time of day it would best for me to pick up grandma from the airport. I begged her to make sure she is definitely coming before she buys her that ticket because I know that Lisa's mom changes her mind more than a Las Vegas showgirl changes her clothes. "No, no" Lisa states "she is coming for sure, she told me." I just wanted to make sure so Lisa did make a call to her mom right before she bought the plane ticket. Guess what? Lisa's mom decided it is not a good time to come. Lisa already told our girls she is coming and they were very excited. All Lisa can do is slam the phone down crying as she now has to turn around and explain somehow to our daughters that Grandma is not coming to visit them. I hate to be right in circumstances such as this one, but I knew she wasn't going to come.

Her excuse wasn't valid and Lisa was livid to say the least. The girls were devastated as now I have a house full of crying women. I had enough and placed a call to Grandma myself. I explained to her that she has no valid reasons not to come and all she is doing is hurting my girls, her daughter and herself. She really didn't explain why she wasn't coming but still decided she wasn't no matter how hard I pleaded my case. I hung up and tried to patch my family back together. Lisa's mom has been known to change her mind and even go to the extremes of canceling holidays because she isn't "in the mood." Every year since I have known Lisa (about 17 years now) Lisa's mom has actually canceled Christmas usually a few days before. But as always, she always changes her mind just in time and Christmas always seems to arrive at Grandma's house. It is now an inside joke within the family as to when Grandma is going to cancel Christmas during the month of December. The problem I had with Lisa's mom not coming to visit is that she wasn't just hurting herself by not coming, she was hurting my family and it made me very upset and angry with her. It took Lisa about 2 weeks before she would even consider talking to her mother again. I didn't blame her, but she is still her mother and sooner or later she would have to talk to her. Time does heal all wounds and about 3 months and numerous phone calls of my begging finally wore her down as Lisa's mom actually has arrived. She is here in person as I type this sentence. Actually the only way I am being able to type this sentence is because the girls are crawling all over her back as I am left alone. She will be here for two weeks. She originally was only going to come for one week, but I insisted and demanded that she come for two weeks to make up for her fumble a few months ago. She said "yes" with no hesitation.

It is now one week into her visit as it has been as close to perfect as a grandma's visit should be. I have always gotten along very well with Lisa's mom. The only problem with her is her mood swings, but hey, nobody can be perfect like me. The girls adore her; as she is a great grandmother. If I looked up the word grandmother in the dictionary, I am sure Lisa's mom would fit that definition like a glove. The only negative of the visit is this is one of those times I wished I worked and Lisa stayed home. Not because I don't get along with Lisa's mom, but so Lisa would be able to spend more time with her mother than the time she is able at night and on the weekends. Lisa has decided that she is going to take a couple of days off the second week to spend more time with her mom. That makes me happy as I think I should be able to squeeze in a round a golf during that time. That would make Daddy very happy. The new golf season has started and every weekend I have been watching golf on TV drooling on myself. I can't wait to hit the little white ball and swear obscenities. Golf, what a game! Anyways, as the girls play with Grandma I am able to do things around the house that I am not usually able to do as I am the one the girls crawl all over. I don't feel too guilty about dumping the girls onto Grandma for a few reasons. One, Grandma doesn't see her granddaughters that much as she needs to soak up as much of McKenzie and Josie and she can in a short period of time. Two, I paid for her to come down her so this is her payback on her plane fare. Three, she is a great grandmother and I know she is having the time of her life. The best thing about having Grandma here is spending time alone with Lisa without the kids. It is amazing how much I miss just being alone with just my wife in peace without any rugrats around. We haven't gone out for the night or anything, just a walk around the block together is paradise to us. Being able to walk out your own door and not have to worry about your children is priceless. All the gold in the world doesn't carry its weight on the feeling of being free from your kids, as you know they are in Grandma's hands. I would like to go out at least one night alone with my wife while Grandma is here. We don't want to take advantage of her, as I believe we haven't. I didn't fly her down her so she can spend every waking moment babysitting. That would be rude and uncalled for as it would take years for her to come back if we did that to her. She helps just by being here making my girls happy. If my girls are happy, that makes Daddy happy, and if Daddy is happy, he will make Mommy happy, and if Mommy is happy, everyone is happy. Who knows, maybe after these two weeks, Lisa's mom will realize how good it is living here and she will want to move down by us. Lisa wants her to, but all of her other family members are still in the Chicago area and it would be hard for her. I don't blame her on that decision, but she does like to visit here when she decides to. After this visit, I believe it won't take much begging to get her to come back. I'll just have to put on my charm and get my girls on the phone as no Grandma would be able to resist the sounds of two lovely children wanting their grandma. Even so, I will have my fingers crossed the whole time.

Snow day

I was able to do something with my daughters that I would never think I would be able to do living in the south: take them sledding. Anything is possible and that holds true to having a snow storm in the south. The meteorologists were predicting a snow storm (But they are wrong more times than they are right so I don't believe anything they ever say) as I thought my eyes were playing tricks on me as we woke up this morning with about 5 inches of snow on the ground. I haven't seen snow in two years and for the first time in a long time I thought it was just beautiful. All the tall trees were covered in white fluffy flakes as the scenery around our house and around the neighborhood looked like a scene out of a Norman Rockwell portrait, absolute beauty. McKenzie was very excited to see the snow as she has been asking me these past two winters "When is it going to snow, Daddy?" I have to keep explaining to her that in the South where we live now, it doesn't snow very often, if ever like it did when we lived in Chicago. I can't blame her for wanting it to snow. When you are a kid snow is a great thing. When you are an adult with children, snow is a bad thing. Kids play in the snow and get off school when there is a snowstorm. Parents have to shovel the snow, drive in the snow and bundle the kids up in layers of clothes. It is such a hassle it is better off just staying inside and not have to deal with it. This was a freak of nature having 5 inches of snow on the ground. Lisa cannot get to work since there is no way she can drive without any snow plows or salt on the road. So what is a father to do? I declared the day a "snow day" and all that was on the agenda was fun!

Josie was very excited since she was too young to remember the snow when she was a baby, but she knows what snow is from television and books. McKenzie remembers what fun snow can be as she can't get out the door fast enough. If I didn't stop her she might have dove right into the snow naked. I myself have to admit that I couldn't wait to get out there as I was excited to play in the snow with my two little snow angels. I unburied the sled from the basement and went across the street to our neighbor's house. Their house is on a hill with a very long driveway that is perfect for sledding on. I am sure when they built their house they would never of imagined someday two little girls and their dad would be snow sledding down it, but that is what was about to happen. Josie was hesitant as she didn't want to do it. McKenzie, who is very brave couldn't wait. I put Josie in the front and McKenzie in the back to hold Josie tight with her arms so she wouldn't be afraid. I pushed them down the driveway with all of my might as they shot down all the way across the street like Olympic bob-sledders. As I rushed down to the bottom of the driveway to welcome them, all I saw was a big huge smile on Josie's face as she repeated "Again, again." Her fear was quickly forgotten. We sledded for about an hour then Josie had enough. She is turning into a true southerner as she had enough of the snow and the cold and wanted to go back into the house where it is warm and dry. I give her credit for hanging in as long as she did. McKenzie on the other hand couldn't get enough of the snow. I asked her if she wanted to go inside and she said "no" emphatically. My daughter and I proceeded to make a snowman along with snow angels on our front lawn. I broke out our dust covered snow shovel to shovel our driveway. Then I had the biggest thrill yet with my proclaimed "snow day," my first snowball fight with one of my own children. I want to be the cool dad and have fun with my children as I pounded my first born with snow. I had no mercy on her as it was my way of paying her back for all the frustration she gives me on any given day. She was covered in snow from her head to her toes, her cheeks were bright red and her teeth were shiny white as they chattered in a frozen state. Even though I got the best of her, she had a huge smile the whole time we had our snowball fight. She made good snowballs and showed off a pretty good throwing arm, but her dad was an old pro as I took her down. I don't know who's smile was bigger, hers or mine. After our snowball fight she helped shovel our driveway like a big girl, then we both decided it was time to finally go inside our warm house for some hot chocolate.

Days like today are what having children is all about. I had the time of my life outside with my daughters playing in the snow. The day was as perfect as a snowflake. The day was filled with fun and laughter, no worries, no schedules, just fun. Days like today don't come around much, so when they do, you must take full advantage of them and drop everything you had planned and just enjoy the day with your children. I said it before, and I will say it again; "Life moves too fast, if you don't stop to get off and enjoy it, you are going to miss it."

Barney Live

Being the great dad I am I took my girls over the weekend to see their hero, Barney. Yes, Barney the big purple singing dinosaur my family has been watching and listening to for the past five years. Barney and his whole gang is touring different cities for a special 2-hour concert. Once I heard that Barney was coming, I had no choice but to get tickets for my daughters so they can see him in person as they have seen him only on the television. I did have to take a second mortgage out on the house to afford buying decent seats, but I knew once Barney came out on stage, the look my daughters will have in their eyes would be worth every penny. I didn't tell my girls we were going until a few days before the event. I didn't want to be bothered with anticipation like I am around Christmas. So I waited to tell them once all the arrangements were made and were final. I can't describe how excited they were when the heard the news, about as excited as I get when Lisa and I have a babysitter and we are able to go out for a night out alone. Both my girls love Barney as I myself don't mind watching the purple beast. Most people say they hate Barney, but deep down inside all of the doubters, I know they all like him too, just like me, but they just don't have the courage to admit it.

As the morning came my girls got all dressed up, as they couldn't wait to get there. When we arrived at the theater where Barney was going to perform, all you could see in front of you were little kids with the look in their eyes knowing soon they will see their best friend in the world, Barney. Even the parents seemed excited as I have to admit I was very excited. I was excited for my daughters as they have been Barney-heads all their lives, and excited for myself as I am going to be the "best dad in the world" when this is all over because I was the one that made this all possible. The theater was a complete sell out as there wasn't an empty seat to be found. I was growing with anticipation as I wanted it to begin so I can see the glee and happiness in my girls faces as soon as Barney appeared on the stage. All of a sudden the lights dimmed as children everywhere begin to scream as a little stuffed purple dinosaur appeared in the center of the stage. My daughters eyes were just hypnotized on t he stuffed animal and then with a flash, Barney appeared larger than life. The look and the excitement from my girls faces were priceless. Just like the credit card commercials: " Barney Live and making your girls happier than ever, priceless." They didn't move through the whole show as they laughed and sang with Barney and his friends all the way to the end. It was a fantastic show as I myself was highly impressed with the production. Every child and every parent sang the "I love You Song" at the end as a tear comes strolling down my face. My daughters love Barney and I was so happy I was able to bring them to see him as they gave me a big kiss and a hug once it was all over and told me that they love me very much. That is the definition of "priceless."

Revenge of the Ebola virus

I don't get sick much, or does the rest of my family. We are in generally a very healthy group, and that's a good thing. Why? Because when sickness strikes the Major family, divorce court isn't far away. One of the worse times I have had staying home raising my daughters is when I am sick. No matter how sick I may be, I have to go on with my day as if I was a 100 percent, even though I am not. The days seem as long as the bible, as I count the minutes until relief comes home from work, that being my wife. I thought it was relief until recently when I came down with "the Ebola virus."

Granted it wasn't truly the "Ebola virus," but it sure felt like it. McKenzie had it first as she gracefully passed it onto me. She ran a high fever for two days and basically laid around the house like a limp noodle. I called the doctor to find out if I needed to bring her in, but I was instructed there is a bad virus going around and unless the fever doesn't break within 3 days, there was really nothing that can be done except wait it out. Wait I did, I waited just enough time until it infected my body with its evil presence. McKenzie did shake it off within 2 days as now it is in my blood stream. The first day I had a fever just over a hundred. I felt like I had a hangover, but I still was able to function at about 75 percent as I pulled at my inner strength to make it through the day. My wife basically gave me no support or comfort thinking I just had a cold and to be a man and deal with it. I don't know why I married her sometimes. I had to remind her about her wedding vows, "in sickness and in health." She just laughed and went on her way. The second day was a whole new ball game. I woke up with a fever over 102 degrees. I was delirious and couldn't see straight. I told my wife I did not feel comfortable driving the kids to school as I can barely walk straight. Being finally convinced I might be sick, since I am not willing to risk my children harm, she stayed home in the morning to drive our girls to school then went to work. I went straight to bed as I thought that Satan has taken over my body. Lisa did leave work during lunch to pick up the girls at school, but left me with them in the afternoon as she returned to work. It took every once of energy I had to make it through the day as the virus took a huge strain on my body because at night I couldn't move off the couch. That is when I began looking in the yellow pages for a divorce attorney. After my wife graciously put our girls to sleep for the night, she began hassling me telling me I was milking my illness and to get my butt off the couch. I lost it! I couldn't believe what my wife was saying. Does she think I am being a slug? I basically told her that she is very insensitive and she had no idea how bad I felt as I went straight upstairs into our bed and locked the door. She tried to apologize but what was said, was said and she couldn't take it back. I know she meant what she said as she wouldn't of said it to begin with if she didn't mean it. However, she and I both didn't know what was in store next. The next day God and my mother in heaven must have been listening because the virus left my body and infiltrated hers. Revenge is a dish better served cold! Whatever that means I don't care, all I know is it was a dished served sweet.

She had all the symptoms I had for the past two days: high fever, soreness, dizziness and basically feeling like a truck just ran over your body. For two days she didn't move off the couch, much like I tried to do. Even though she was sick and miserable, I took care of her like I wanted to be taken care of but wasn't for two reasons. One, I know how she felt as I wanted to make her comfortable. Second, I let her know how wrong she was assuming that I was milking my illness as she laid there in agony. She apologized profusely as I did my best to comfort her, but it did all come with sarcasm and ridicule from me. I did not feel sorry for her as she was being punished from above for her own wrong doing when I was sick.

After a few days the Major family was once again at 100 percent. It was weird how Josie never caught the virus as I counted my blessings. If she would of gotten sick, it would have been ugly. She does not take illness well and she is the smallest as I wouldn't know how bad the "Ebola virus" would of effected her. My wife now promises as long as she lives that she will never act the way she did when I was sick as she states she will never take my illnesses lightly again. She learned a valuable lesson this week as life was on my side. Call it fate, irony, Murphy's Law, whatever fits, but when my wife got sick, the one thing she did a lot of was eating, she ate a lot of crow!

New arrival

It's a girl! I can't believe I did it again. I guess I haven't learned my lesson, as I am a gluten for punishment. When is enough is enough? My wife has been begging me, my daughters have been begging me, and to be honest I have been thinking about it a lot lately. Ever since McKenzie has been going to school everyday, along with Josie twice a week, I often found myself very lonely in the house. I have plenty of chores to do, but I do them alone. It is a weird feeling that comes over you as there are days when the house is in such chaos and out of control as you can't even hear yourself think straight, as you would kill for one minute to be left alone in peace and quiet. When I do have that time, when they are both at school, I am missing the girls more than I would like to admit. McKenzie only goes to school 4 hours a day now, but next year it will be a full eight to nine hour day. Josie will be bumped up to three days a week. What will I do? Get a job? No way, I must think of something else to do to be able to stay at home and not enter the rat race all over again. The money would come in handy but I enjoy staying home too much to go back to a cubical. So what is a person to do? One way to secure myself to staying at home is by adding to the family. I would prefer to have another girl as that is what I am accustom to. I wouldn't know how to handle a boy, so a girl is what I prefer. I did a lot of soul searching before I came to the decision to add another being in this world that I am solely responsible to care and nurture for. But I decided it was best for me and my family. Last Saturday as I drove around by myself pondering my decision, I stopped at the local mall to secure my thoughts. As I approached the window to one of the most beautiful creatures I have ever laid eyes on (besides my two lovely daughters) I wiped out my credit card and purchased my new headache and pain in the ass. Her name is Shadow, a Siberian Husky puppy that has her Daddy's eyes and her mother's looks.

Pet peeves

Being the outstanding parent I am (if not the best parent in the world) I have three pet peeves that I have towards other parents that I have to get off my chest. I'm not saying I am perfect, but I do come close. My three pet peeves are things that should be taken for granted, automatically done being a care giver, but I often see them sided for some reason or another. Let me explain my three things that make the hair on my neck stand straight up.

Runny noses that do not get wiped in a timely manner. I see children all the time with green muck draining out their noses, onto their upper lip without the courtesy of a wipe from their mother or father within reasonable time. It makes me sick just thinking about it. Your child has a cold, fine, be prepared with a handkerchief or tissue and wipe your child's nose once in a while before they gross out everyone they come in contact with. It literally makes my stomach turn when I see a child with snot on their face without anyone wiping it off immediately as it leaves a nostril. As soon as either of my girls have a runny nose and needs a wipe, I am there as soon as any runny oozements escapes their nostrils. The only thing worse than not wiping a child's runny nose is a child eating their boogers. That's another story I don't even want to get into because I might have to throw up as that is about as disgusting as anyone can possibly get. If your hungry, eat a cookie, not a booger. Gross!

Unsupervised children. Whenever I go somewhere with my children, I watch them like a hawk. I always keep my eye on them and I am within distance of them if something bad was to happen, I am there close enough that I believe I can spare some of the damage that might occur. Children are too small to be left unattended for even a fraction of a second. I don't think I was left alone until I was 16 years old. The world is a very dangerous place and bad things can happen to those putting themselves into a bad situation. Not watching or supervising your children at all times gives you better odds for something to go wrong without you there to prevent it from happening.

Children that are not in car seats. Whenever I am driving and I see babies or small children not strapped in car seats, it drives me crazy. I feel like pulling over the driver and totally lashing out at them regarding the safety of their children and the dangers of not having them in a car seat. Not only can you protect your child from serious injury if in fact you get into an accident while driving, but could possibly save them from death. I have been a firm believer in making sure my children are strapped in at all times. I don't have to worry about my driving as much as I have to worry about every other speed racer out there trying to get somewhere five seconds faster than the next person. People drive like every road is the Indianapolis 500 racetrack. Why? Who knows, everyone is in a hurry to go nowhere. I have witnessed infants being held by their mother or father in the front seat while driving on the highway. If that driver was to get into an accident, the odds of that infant surviving are slim. Why punish that innocent baby for your own laziness or cheapness in not strapping that baby in infant carrier where it belongs. At times I wish I was a cop. I would pull everyone over whenever I saw anyone not having their children strapped in and throw the maximum fine at them that I could. I would even try to throw them in jail to get my point across. When you are a parent you need to be responsible and not having your babies in car seats is not being a responsible parent. You are playing Russian Roulette not having your children fastened securely while driving, and that is one game you don't want to lose.

Fighters, please return to your corners

The sibling rivalry has arrived with a bang. I have been waiting in anticipation for this and I am not being disappointed. Part of the fun of having children in my eyes is the power struggle that goes on between siblings, especially when they are close in age such as my daughters. They basically have the same interests and desires so there are many battles among the two of them when one doesn't get her way with the other. McKenzie has been given a trait that must have been passed on by me: antagonist. She is very good at it, as I am, as she just pesters her little sister until she can't take it anymore. She knows exactly what buttons to push on Josie to get her upset. After she gets Josie upset, I can see a smile form on her face as she knows she has done what she has set out to do. McKenzie does get the best of Josie right now since she is two years older than her and is bigger than her. Also, Lisa and I protect Josie more being that Josie is the "little sister." Even so,

McKenzie still pushes the envelope when it comes to picking on Josie. Josie basically screams or cries whenever something doesn't go her way as I have to intervene to correct the situation. Most of the time Josie gets her way because I can't tolerate her screaming and crying. Mckenize is good about it as she just calls Josie "a cry baby" and leaves her alone. McKenzie doesn't mind as she proves to herself once again she was able to bully her little sister. McKenzie has fun at it and I have fun watching it as long as it doesn't go to far and give me a headache. When I get a headache, all the fun is over and no one picks on any one, anymore that day.

There have been punches thrown, not by McKenzie, but by Josie. McKenzie would never hit Josie, as she knows hitting is not allowed, plus she realizes she is much bigger than Josie and it would not be fair. However, if McKenzie picks on Josie on a bad day, Josie has been known to take a swing at McKenzie to leave her alone. McKenzie immediately tells me that Josie hit her as Josie just looks at me with her big blue eyes as all I can do is smile back at her as I try to explain that hitting her sister is a big "no, no." What I really want to tell her is "good job" and if she bothers you again, whack her harder.

My brother was four years older than me and always beat me and picked on me. I basically took it because he was so much bigger than I was. Finally, I caught up to him in time, and actually passed him up in size as now he talks to me instead of punching me. There will be some knock down, drag out fights between Josie and McKenzie. It is part of nature with two girls, who are two years apart, and are living under the same roof. Battle lines will be drawn as the war between siblings will be fierce and often. I will be the one to pick up the pieces, as I will have to separate them before they kill one another. No matter who is right, or who is wrong, Daddy will be the one to try to explain that they are sisters and that they are also best friends so fighting is not the answer. After the dust clears and the tears dry up, all will be normal again as siblings fight to show their love for one another. My brother and I are closer now than ever before. I have been thinking of a way to profit from all this fighting. I am thinking of selling the fights to t he local cable company by means of pay per view. Everyone loves a good fight in America and what better than two sisters fighting over something stupid. I will make millions.

What the future may hold:

Even though my daughters are only going on the young ages of 3 and 5 years old, I have a pretty good idea what their future may have in store for

189

them. Here a few predictions I foresee.

My first born, McKenzie:

McKenzie is my shining star. She will always be the pot of gold at the end of the rainbow. She is to me, and to many others, a perfect little girl. She listens, she loves school, she is smart, beautiful, athletic and very sensitive. Even though I might be having the worst day possible, she can always turn my day into a great day by just being McKenzie.

In the future, I can see her having straight A's on all her report cards, thus always being on the honor roll. She will be heavily involved in extra curricular activities, such as sports, cheerleading, social clubs and have many, many friends. She will be the prom queen not because she wanted to but because everyone else will want her to be. She will have many years of perfect attendance at school being she loves school that much. Boys will be a problem, not for her, but for me. She will be the "it" girl as every male body within miles will want to get "it." That is where I will step in and make sure no one will get "it," believe that! McKenzie will be taught at a very early age the way to handle boys. If she won't be able to handle the boys knocking down our doors, I know I will be able to step in and resolve the situation. She will go to college and I won't have to pay for it. She will receive a scholarship either from academics or from athletics. She is that talented. I don't want to label her as a gifted child, but she is very close to that distinction.

I see her graduating college with a real degree, not just a "Mrs." degree that many girls go to college for. It will be in astrophysics or biology, something very tough. The reason I believe this is that McKenzie idolizes her mother so much already, I believe she will want to follow in her mother's footsteps and take control of her own life and not have to rely on anyone to have to take care of her. She will be able to take care of herself. That is what McKenzie's mom has done, McKenzie will feel like she must do the same. She already talks about how she is going to go to work someday just like her "Mommy" does. No matter what she decides to do, she will be nothing but successful at it.

She will marry a very handsome man, just like her Mommy did. She will have a large family consisting of four children and a dog. I don't see her moving far away from us or her sister. I know that she won't move far from her sister because her sister will more than likely be living with her, but I will have my thoughts on Josie next. I will need to be close by for babysitting as McKenzie goes off to "save the world" from whatever the world needs to be saved from. That will be ok by me if that is what it is going to take for me not to having to "save the world". I want my daughters close by Lisa and I and not far away, especially when grandchildren start popping out of their bellies. McKenzie will live a long and prosperous life. I am not worried one bit about what the future may hold for McKenzie. Lisa and I will do everything in our power to make sure she has all the opportunity in the world possible to do anything she sets her pretty blue eyes to accomplish. She has her biggest fan in her corner, her father. I will be there with her every step of her life to guide her into being the best McKenzie Major ever put on the face of the earth. All her dreams will come t rue, she will make sure of it, and if she can't for some reason, I will make them all come true.

My second daughter

Josie was put on this earth for a reason; God wants me to see my hair turn gray and fall out at an early age. Josie is completely opposite of McKenzie in almost every way. They are only 23 months apart. They are being raised exactly in the same manner, but Josie does things completely different than McKenzie ever has. She will have get used to hearing how "McKenzie did this" and "how McKenzie did that" because following in McKenzie's footsteps is going to be a hard act to follow.

Josie has been different from her sister since the first minute she arrived on this planet. McKenzie's birth was fairly simple, Josie's birth rather difficult. That is how I see Josie's future: Josie being rather difficult. She will push the limits, and keep Lisa and I constantly on our toes. She is a very stubborn child as she gets that from her mother. Actually she gets it from me but I am too stubborn to admit it. She is tough and mean, but cute at the same time. I always tell her if she wasn't so damn cute, she would be living under the house and not in it.

School will be difficult for her. Not because she isn't smart, but because she has to follow "the golden child," McKenzie. She will always be judged based on what McKenzie has accomplished as Josie will begin to resent that prejudice within time. School will just be a place she has to go to everyday and it won't mean very much to her. She will get decent grades, but nothing to write home about. She won't be in clubs and definitely will not be a cheerleader. I do see her taking auto shop in high school so she can learn to hot-wire a car. Josie will serve her share of detentions, as she won't be a troubled student, just a student who gets into a little trouble from time to time. The principal of her high school and I will be on a first name basis as my phone number will surely be on his or her speed dial. She will graduate high school just because of her last name being Major. If she has the same teachers McKenzie will of had, I am sure they will question me if she is an adopted child.

After high school she will decide to move to Los Angeles and start a rock and roll band. I will not allow her to as she will not be able to move as she will have no money. Josie will not work through high school, instead all she will do is read in her room and listen to some weird music all the time. Instead of moving to Los Angeles she does eventually move out of the house. She moves in with the only other person that I would allow her to move in with, her big sister McKenzie. No matter what will happen in life, McKenzie and Josie will always be there for one another. McKenzie's husband is irate about Josie moving in, but McKenzie basically tells him, "Josie is moving in and if you want, you can move out." He decides to stay which is a good choice on his part.

Josie never does get a job, but instead stays locked in her room at her sister's house as she tries not to interfere with McKenzie's life and her family. I am hard on her as I lecture her and ask her, "Why can't she be more like her sister?" We get into a terrible fight as she goes off into the deep end and explains to me that she is ready to kill herself since all she heard her whole life is, "Why McKenzie you be more like your sister?" She then cries out that "I am not my sister, I am Josie!" She storms out of my sight and I don't see or talk to her for fourteen months.

One day when I am watching the Chicago Cubs try to play baseball, the doorbell rings. Standing there with her arms behind her back and a huge smile on her face is my darling daughter Josie. I am speechless as she tells me she has something to give me. I prayed it was a hug, but instead it is a small wrapped square in the size of a book. I am very puzzled as I begin to open it to find out it is a book. The book is entitled, "Why can't you be more like your sister?" I am puzzled, very puzzled as I stare at this book trying to figure out why my daughter is giving me this book. Then my heart falls from my chest and into my throat as I read the author's name on the front cover of the book: written by Josie Major. My jaw drops to the ground and tears flow from my eyes as I grab a hold of my daughter with both arms hugging her as I tell her two things, "I am sorry and I love you very much." The book becomes a best seller on the New York Times Best Seller List as Josie becomes an instant celebrity. She meets and falls in love with an executive who worked with her on getting her book published. They eventually marry and move to New York together to be closer to their work. Josie goes on to write four more best sellers as she is a huge success. They have two children, both of them boys. She has her hands full as she calls me on the phone almost daily asking for advice on how to control them. I just laugh and basically tell her to take it one day at a time as everything will work out in the end. To reassure everything would work itself out, I remind her that I once had two small children and now look at life and how they turned out. Before I hang up the phone, I tell her two more things: "I love her very much, and how glad she is not like her sister."

My final thoughts

Destiny: 1: Something to which a person or thing is destined: 2: a predetermined course of events often held to be an irresistible power or agency. According to the Webster's Dictionary, that is the definition to the word destiny. With that definition being true, I was destined to be a stay home dad. I was an average student. I hated working in the workforce, and I love my daughters more than anything in this world. To me, becoming a stay home dad was never a decision I had to make; it was my destiny from the beginning of my existence.

Nothing can prepare a person to be a stay home parent except for the love they can give to their children, and the children giving the love back to their parents. That is what life is all about. I didn't know what life was all about until I began staying home with my daughters as they taught me. They have opened my eyes to a world that I didn't know existed. This world that I live in can only be seen by people who are the brave and lucky, to be able to stay home and raise their children without the help or need for daycare. In this day and age, it is getting harder and harder for people to make a good living for themselves and provide their families with the basic needs on only one income. More and more families have to rely on dual incomes, thus meaning their children have no choice but to be put into some sort of a daycare. That makes me extremely sad as I feel so privileged that everyday I get to see my babies grow into the mold that I shape for them. I am blessed, as I thank god almost daily for my daughters who have given me a life that I cannot ever repay them back for. I don't care what the stock market does, I don't care what the interests rates are, I only care where I can buy that new baby doll that actually goes potty and spits up. Why? Because that is what world I live in and I am perfectly happy to be in it.

I was at my daughters preschool today for "hot dogs with dad" since Father's Day is just around the corner. The school wanted to celebrate Father's Day early since school will be out in June when father's day actually occurs. Before we began eating, one of the teachers read a short story that really touched my heart because the story in which she told reminds me of the love my daughters bring to me. The story was of a girl who very much loved her father. One day before Christmas she decided to wrap her own present

Mark S. Major

without the help from anyone else. She unintentionally used the most expensive gold wrapping paper used only for expensive, important Christmas gifts. Most of the wrapping paper was wasted and needed to be thrown away. The father was very upset with his daughter as he scolded her for being so careless and thoughtless explaining to her that money was tight and she needs to be more careful. The daughter tried to explain to her father that she just wanted her present to look perfect, as the present she wrapped was for him. The father then apologized to his daughter and felt horrible for scolding her. When Christmas came the daughter was so excited to give her present to her father she could hardly wait. As soon as she woke up in the morning, she rushed into her father's bedroom and gave her father the present, the same present she was scolded at for wasting all the good wrapping paper. The father open the box and much to his surprise there was nothing in the box, nothing at all. The father was puzzled and angry once again explained to his daughter that when giving someone a present there needs to be an actual present, and not just an empty box pretending to be a present. The daughter then quickly explained that there is something in the box. The box was filled with her love as she put hundreds of kisses inside the box for him so when he felt sad or depressed, to reach inside the box and take some of the love she had have for him to make himself feel better. The father then fell to his knees and began to cry with joy, as he felt his daughter's love as all he can do is hug his daughter and tell her how much he loves her. He then placed the box under his bed for as long as he could remember and whenever he needed cheering up after a bad day, he would open his daughter's box as a smile and tear would always appear on his face. That is the same love and happy feeling my daughters have given me since I have been blessed to be able to stay home and raise my own daughters. This journal I have wrote will stay under my bed, much like the box of kisses, as when I have a bad day, or when one of them spills milk on the carpet as I raise my voice in disgust, I will simply read a few pages as I am sure a smile and a tear will appear on my cheek as I will remember all the love my daughters have given to me. To McKenzie and Josie, Daddy loves you very much.